Branding The Bug

Photography
By:

Vikki Correll

Produced By:

Crooks Gap Photography

ISBN-13:
978-1518888304

ISBN-10:
1518888305

Vikki Correll can be reached for comment at vikkicorrell@gmail.com or
https://www.facebook.com/CrooksGapPhotography.
Her travels and adventures can be followed at https://crooksgapphotography.wordpress.com/ A
wide selection of Vikki's photography can be seen an purchased at:
http://fineartamerica.com/profiles/vikki-correll.html

Cover photos are the property of Vikki Correll
Cover build by:
Crystianna Crawford of
Not A Brown Paper Sack

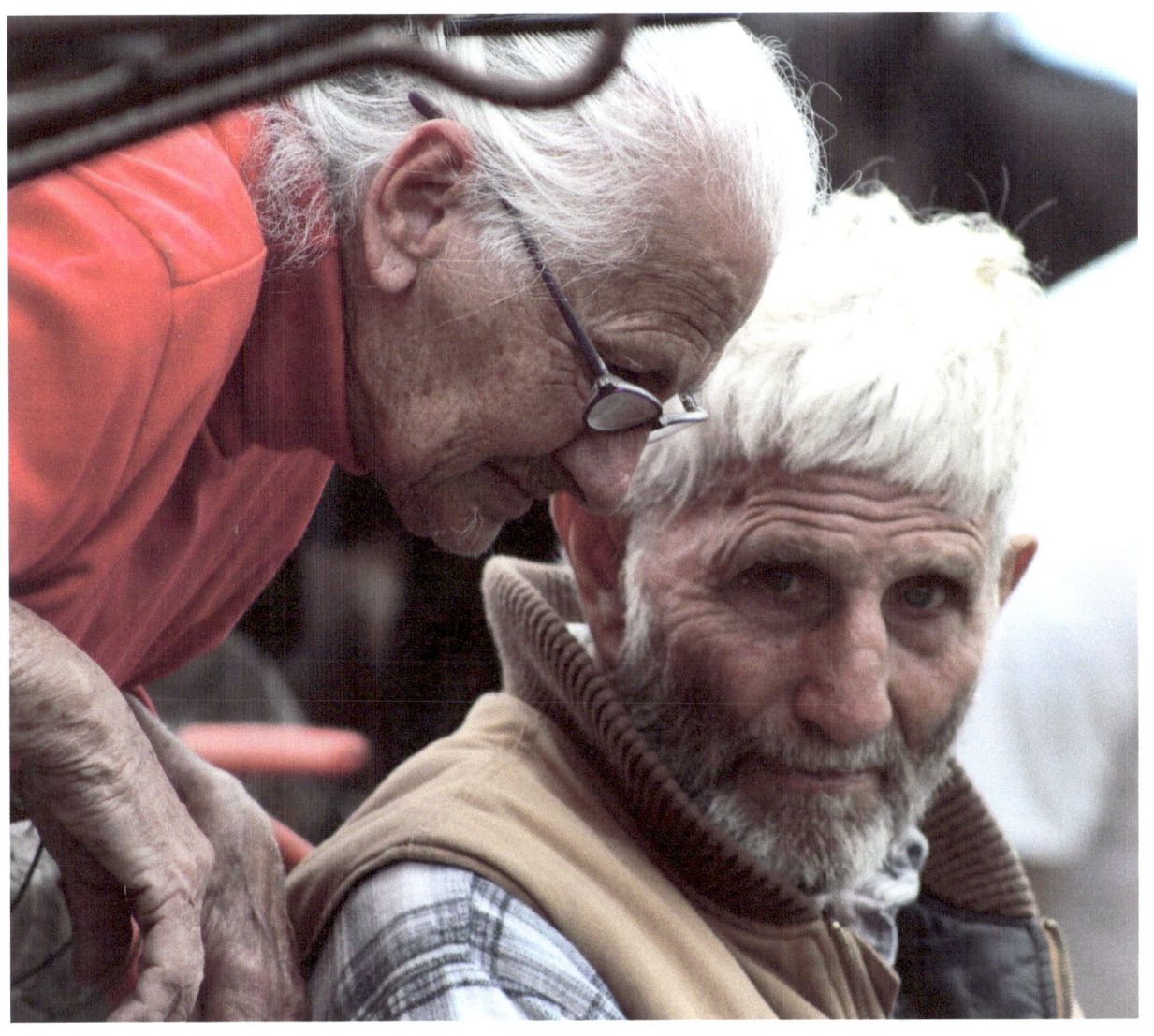

This book is dedicated to Corliss and Glenda Peters, who have devoted their lives to keeping Wyoming's cattle industry thriving. Thank you.

Cattle ranchers are not folk who have a lot of free time – you're not apt to run into them sun bathing on the beach in Mexico or touring the fjords of Norway. Not to say that this isn't possible if planned well; it just isn't likely. Raising and caring for a herd of cattle is pretty much a full time job. They're wild animals, but not in the self-sufficient manner of, say, a bobcat. They will, if given even the slightest chance, get themselves stuck in a mud hole, a gully or a fence, and will often die there if they're not rescued.

The weather in Wyoming can be extreme. A rancher needs to break the ice in winter so that the cows can have water; take them feed every day when the snow is too deep for them to forage; mend the fences that keep them off the highway. Calves born in the bitter cold and snow can often be found in a rancher's kitchen near the stove until they're sound enough to survive outside.

I say all of that to help the reader understand the branding process. It is more than just putting an ownership mark on an animal, although that does help at times – when a neighbor discovers a few cows playing on the highway, endangering not only themselves but the passing motorists, it is handy to be able to call the rancher to whom they belong and effect a rescue.

A branding, though, is a means of checking on the health of both the mother and her babe. While the calves are down to be branded, they're inoculated, checked for open wounds or any other malady that may need tending to, their ears may be tagged for identification more detailed than just the brand. Those male calves that don't have a future as a breeding bull, will be castrated, and if they need to be dehorned, this is when it takes place. Folks gather from surrounding ranches, and sometimes from the bigger cities, to help each other get the job done.

This book contains just a few photos of the branding process as it happened in June of 2015 on The Bug Ranch, in central Wyoming.

This was a satisfying day's work.

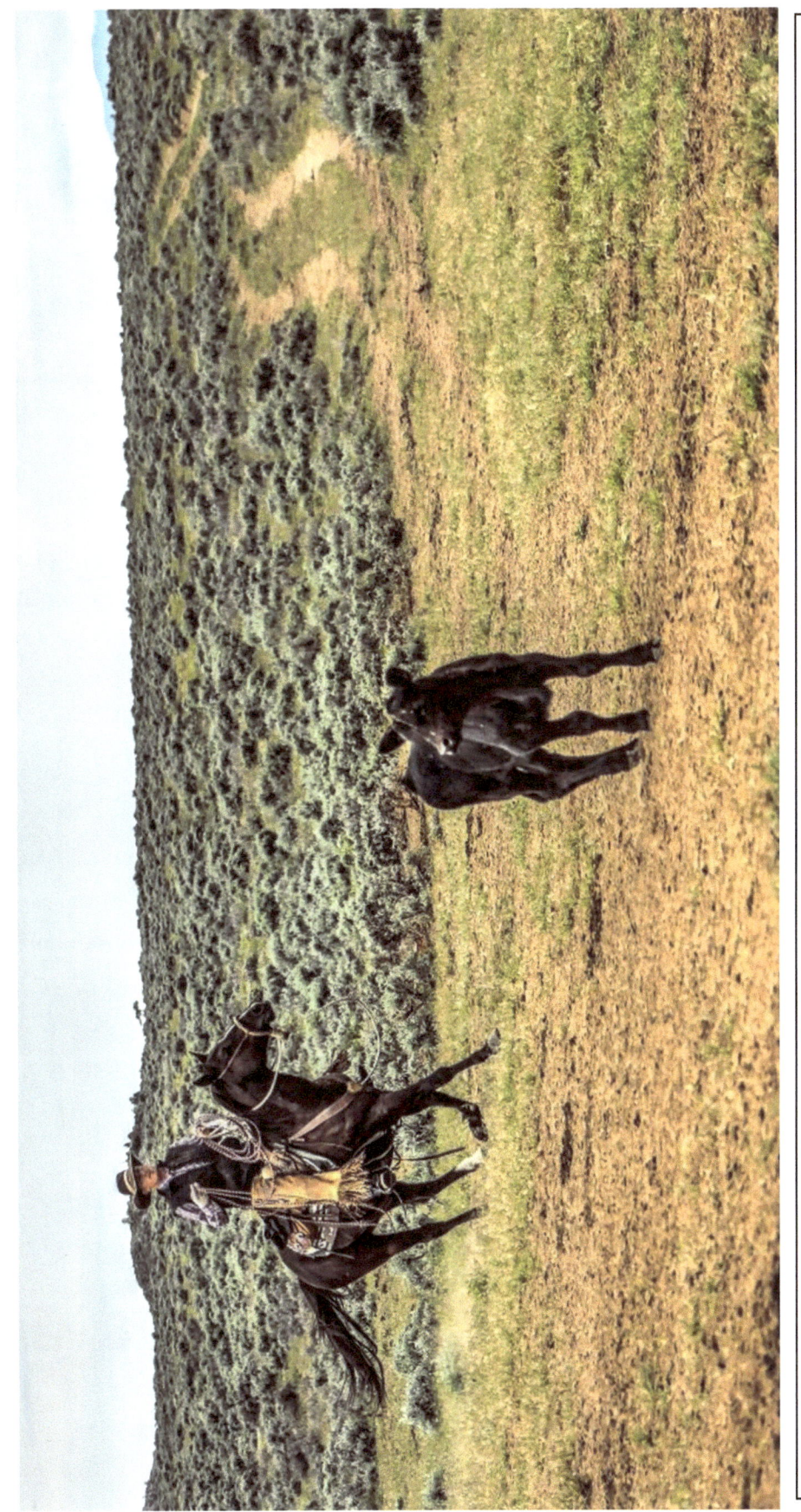

Gathering up that last wandering calf …

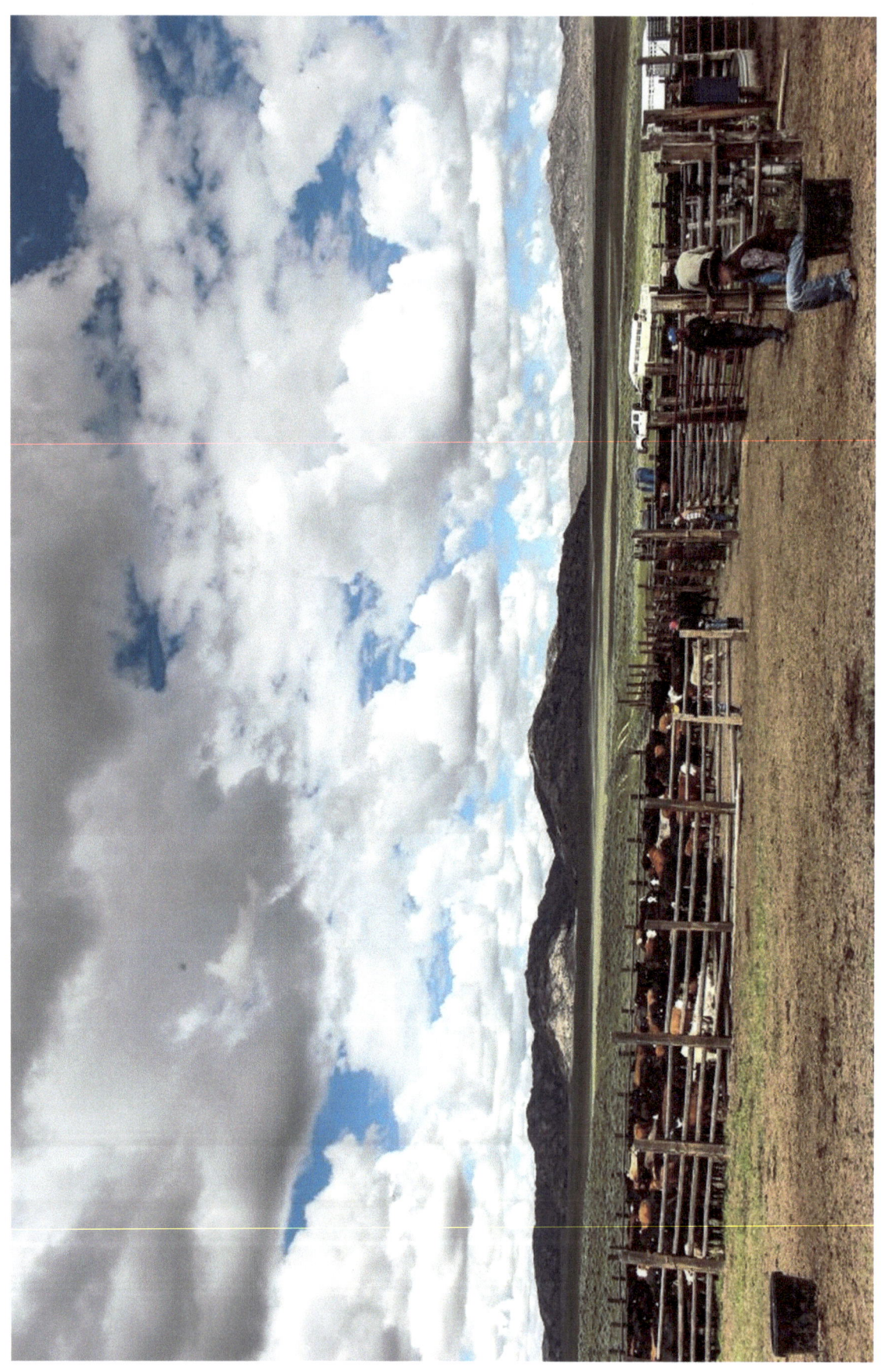

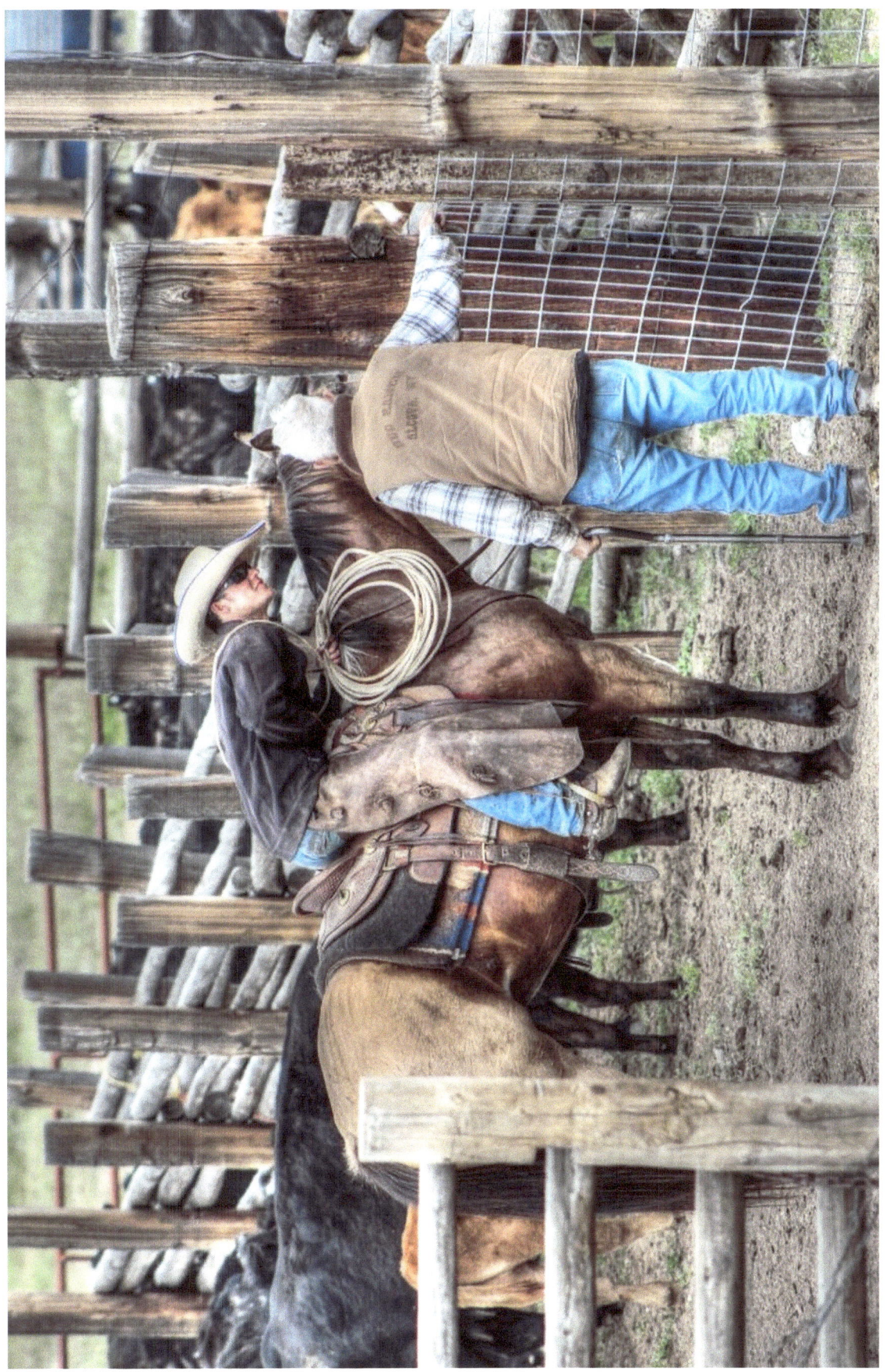

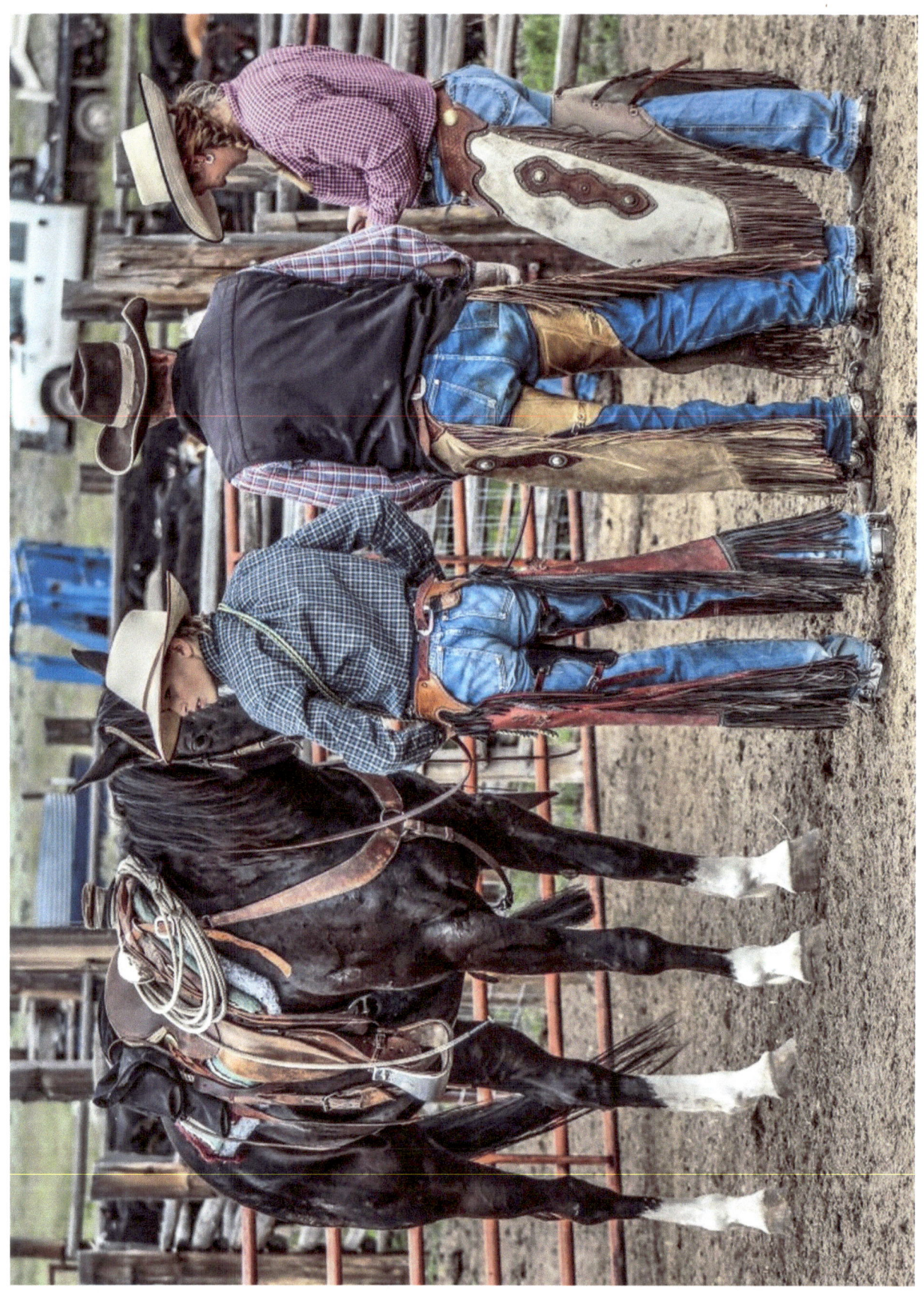

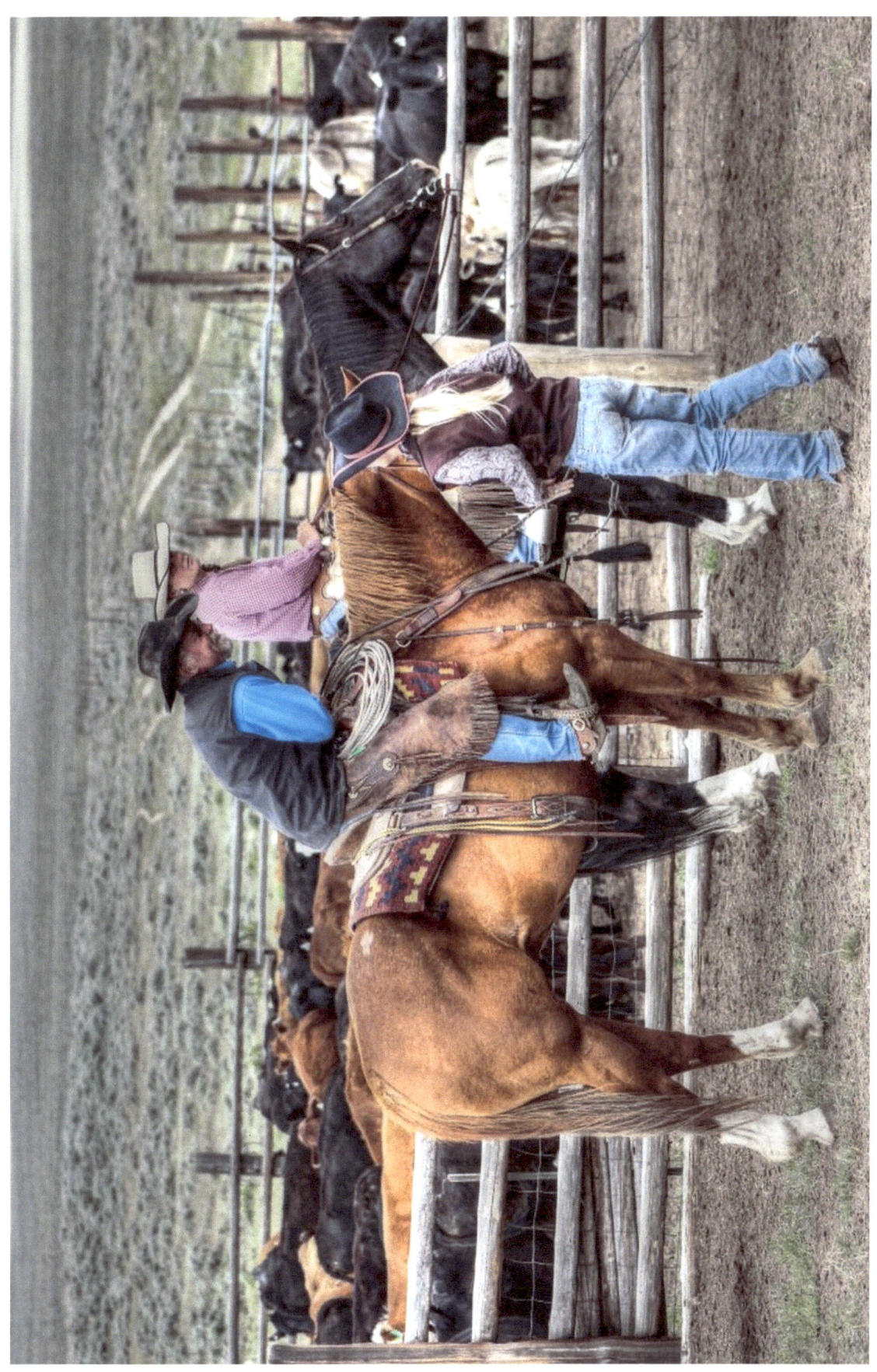

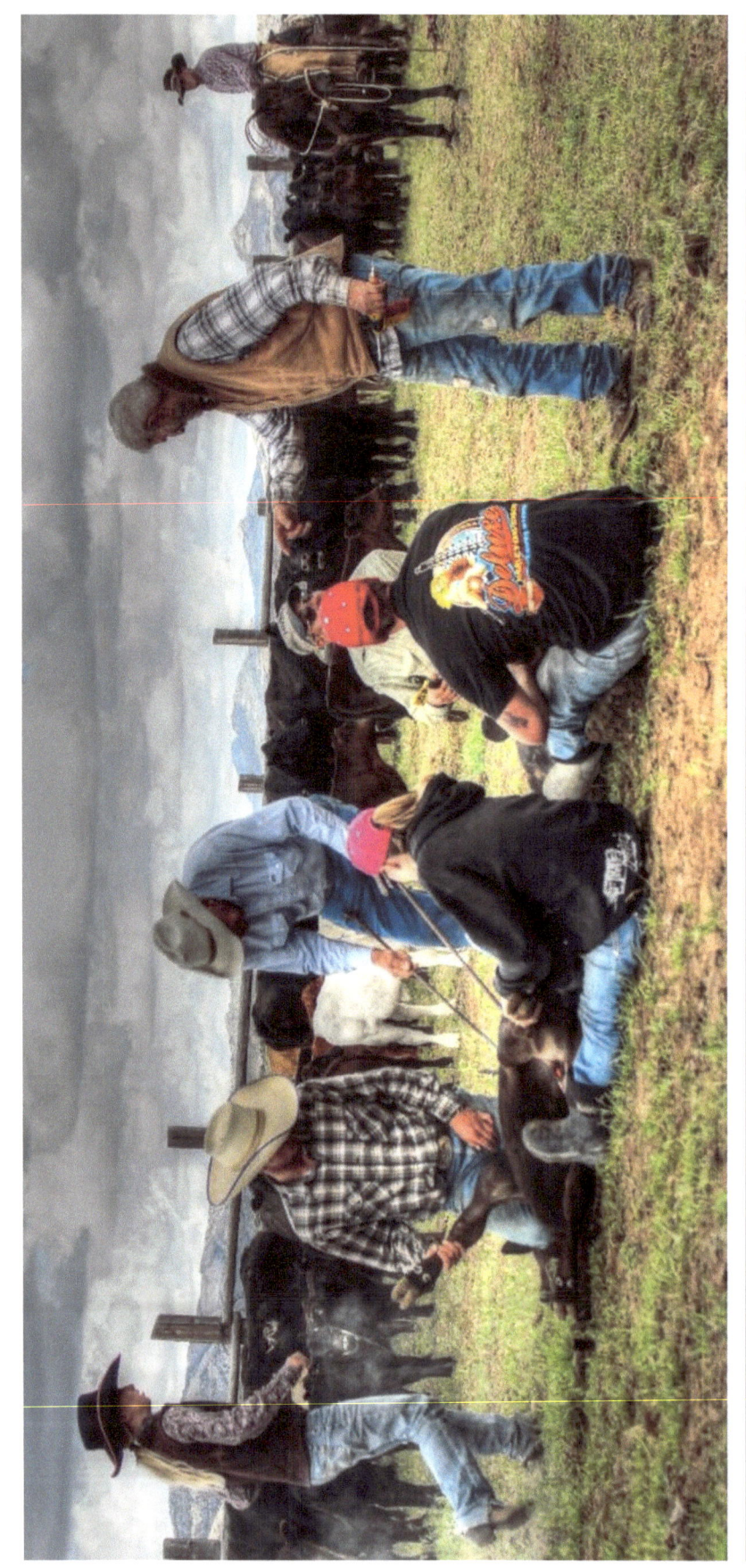

Everyone does whatever job that they see needs doing at the time.

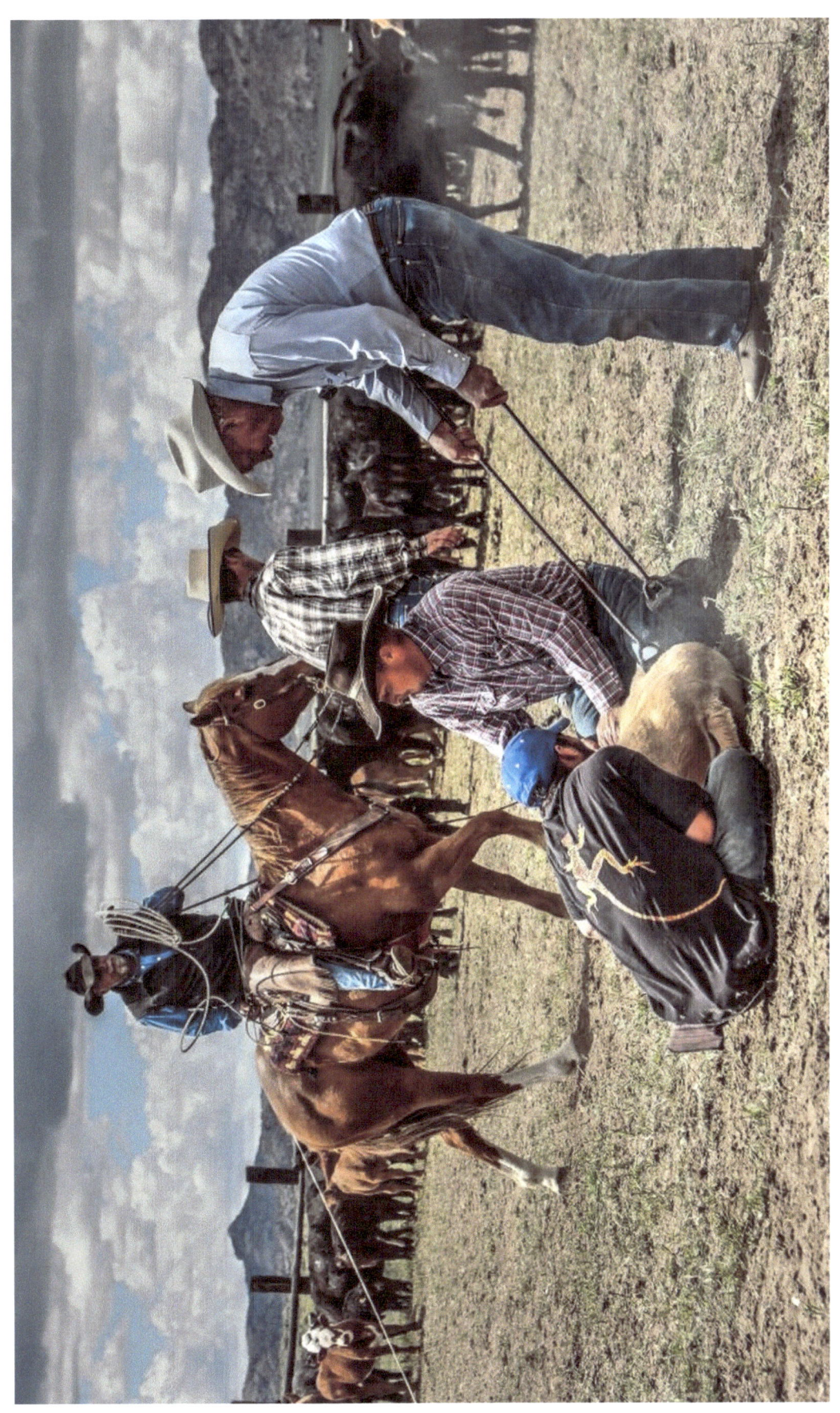

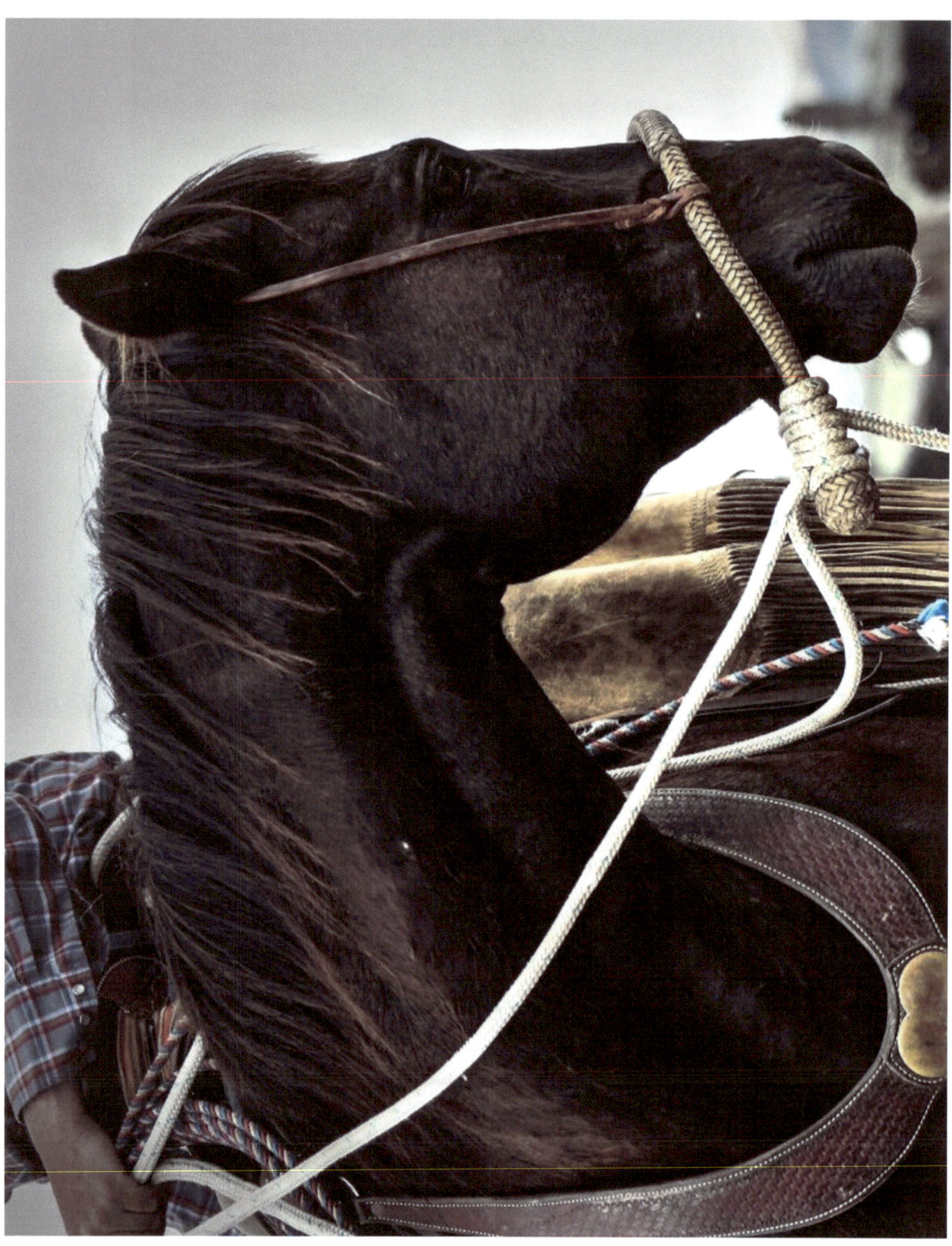

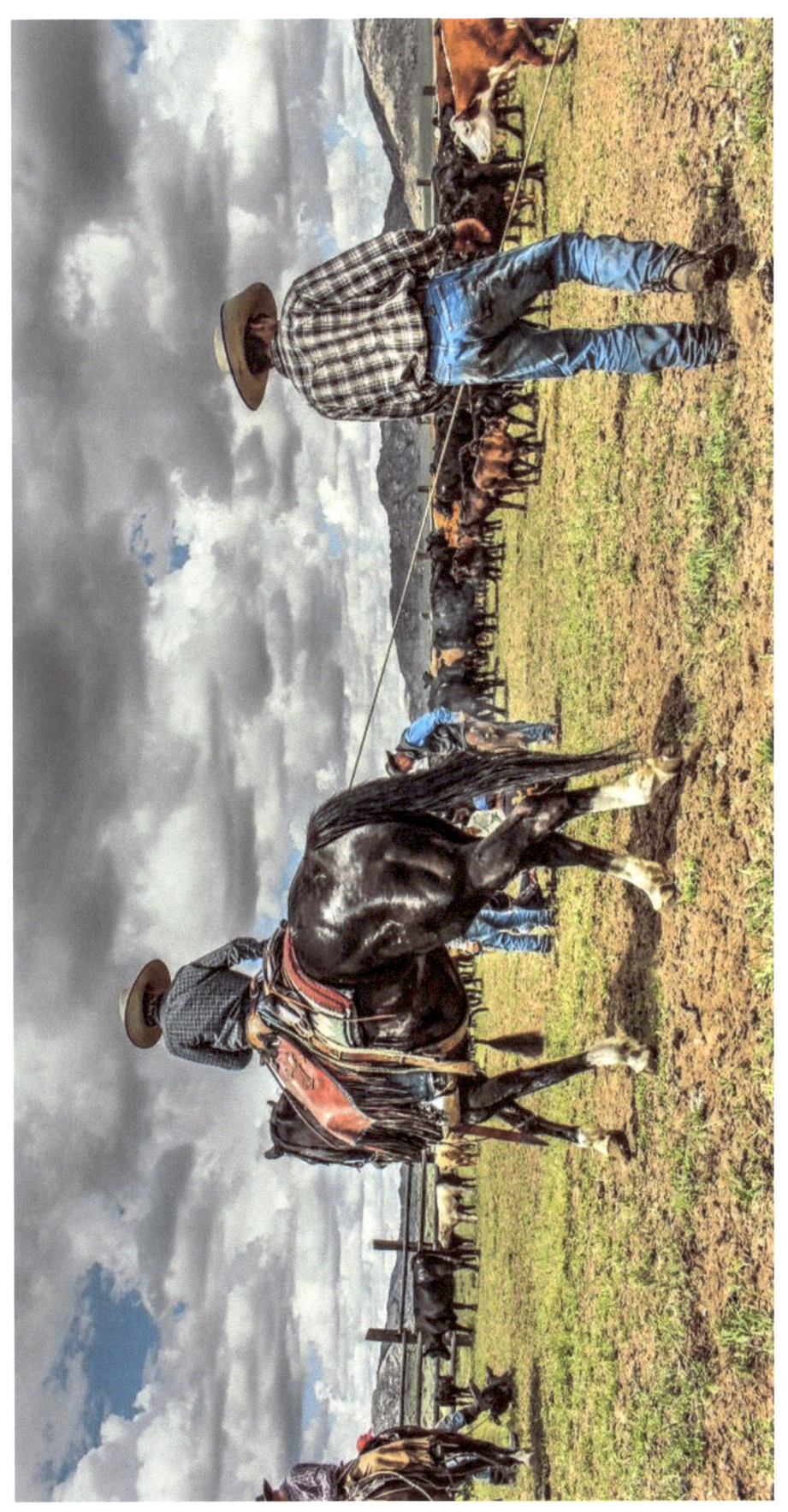

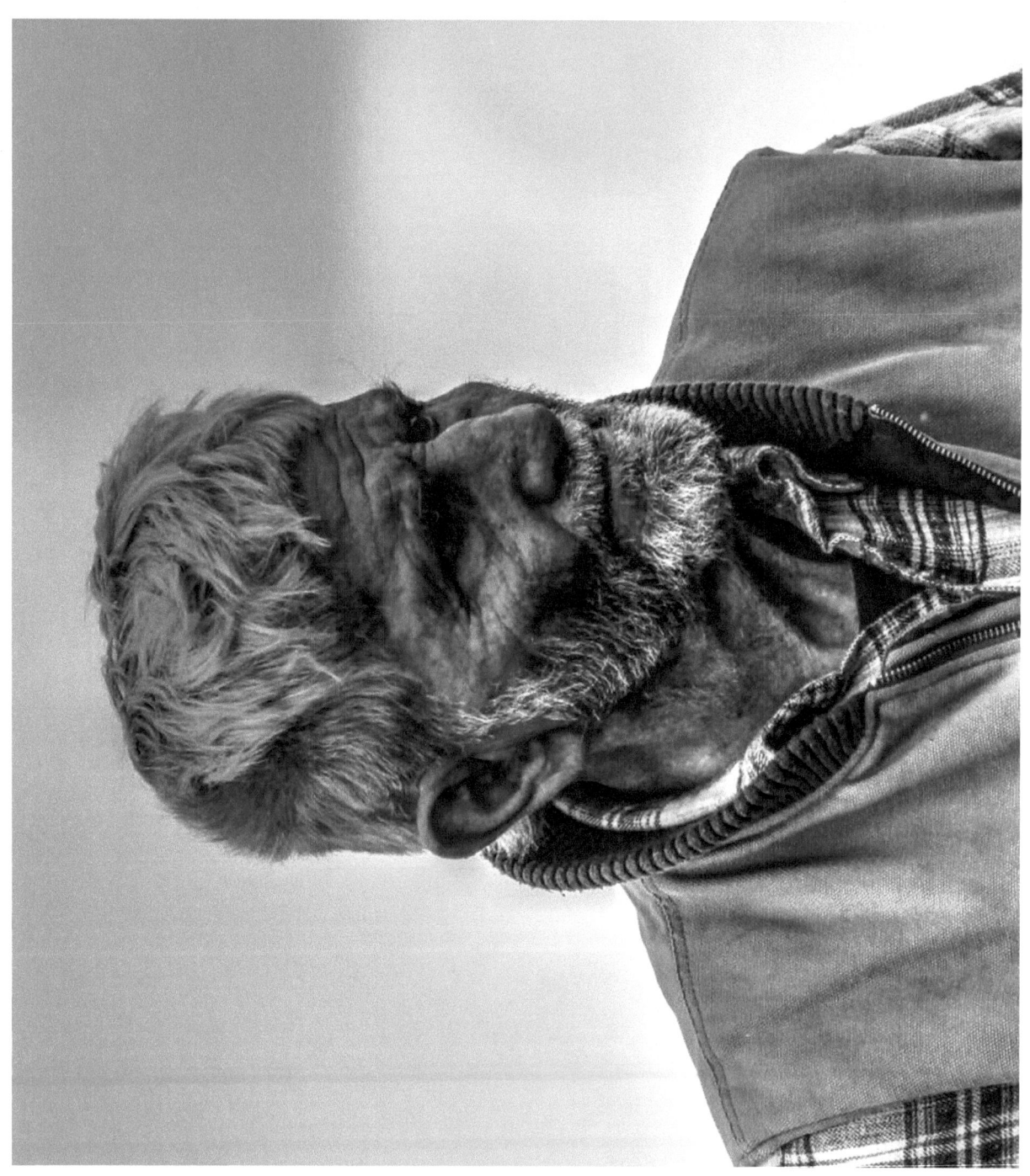

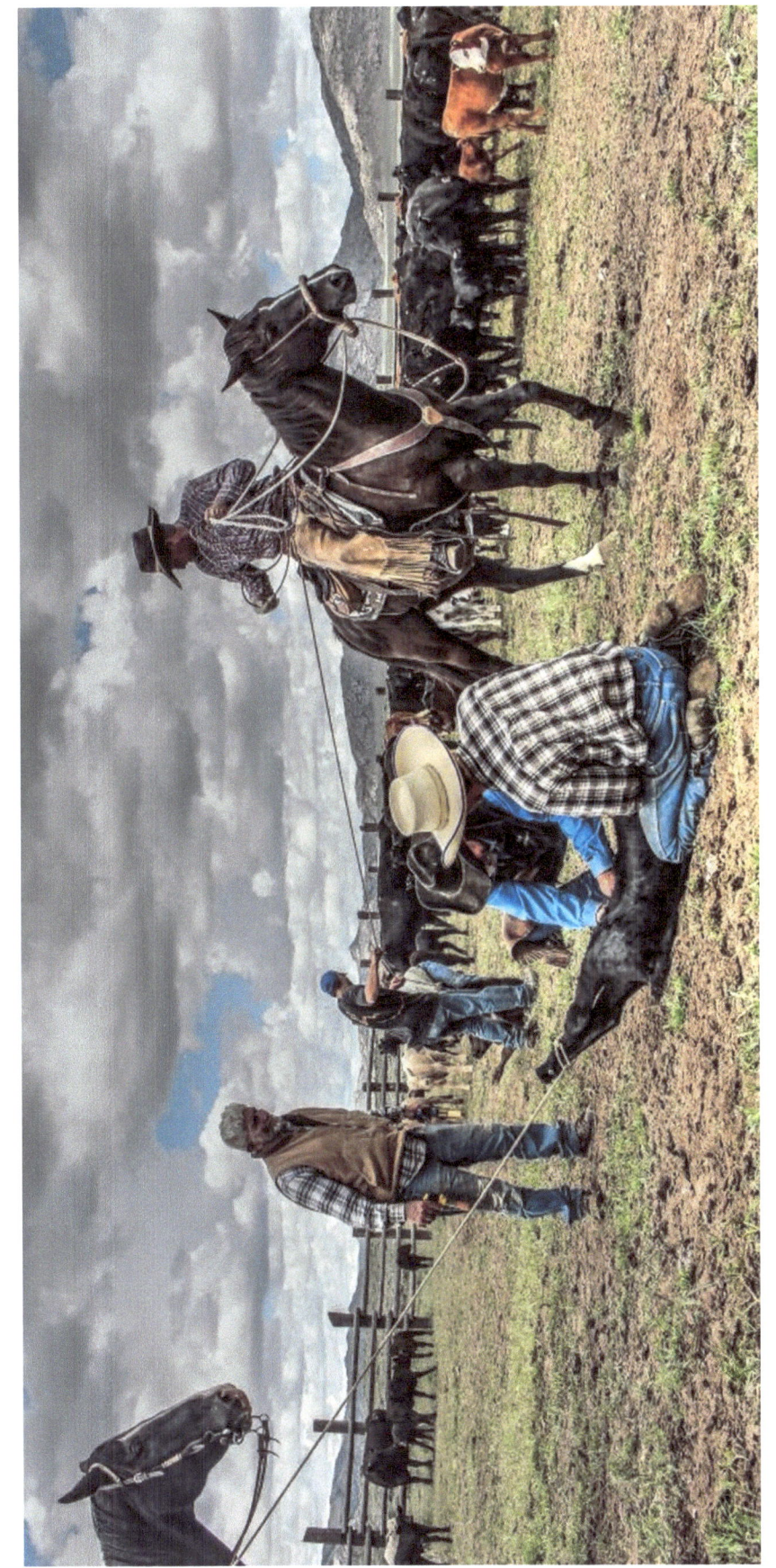

A crew accustomed to working together can get the job done without confusion or chaos.

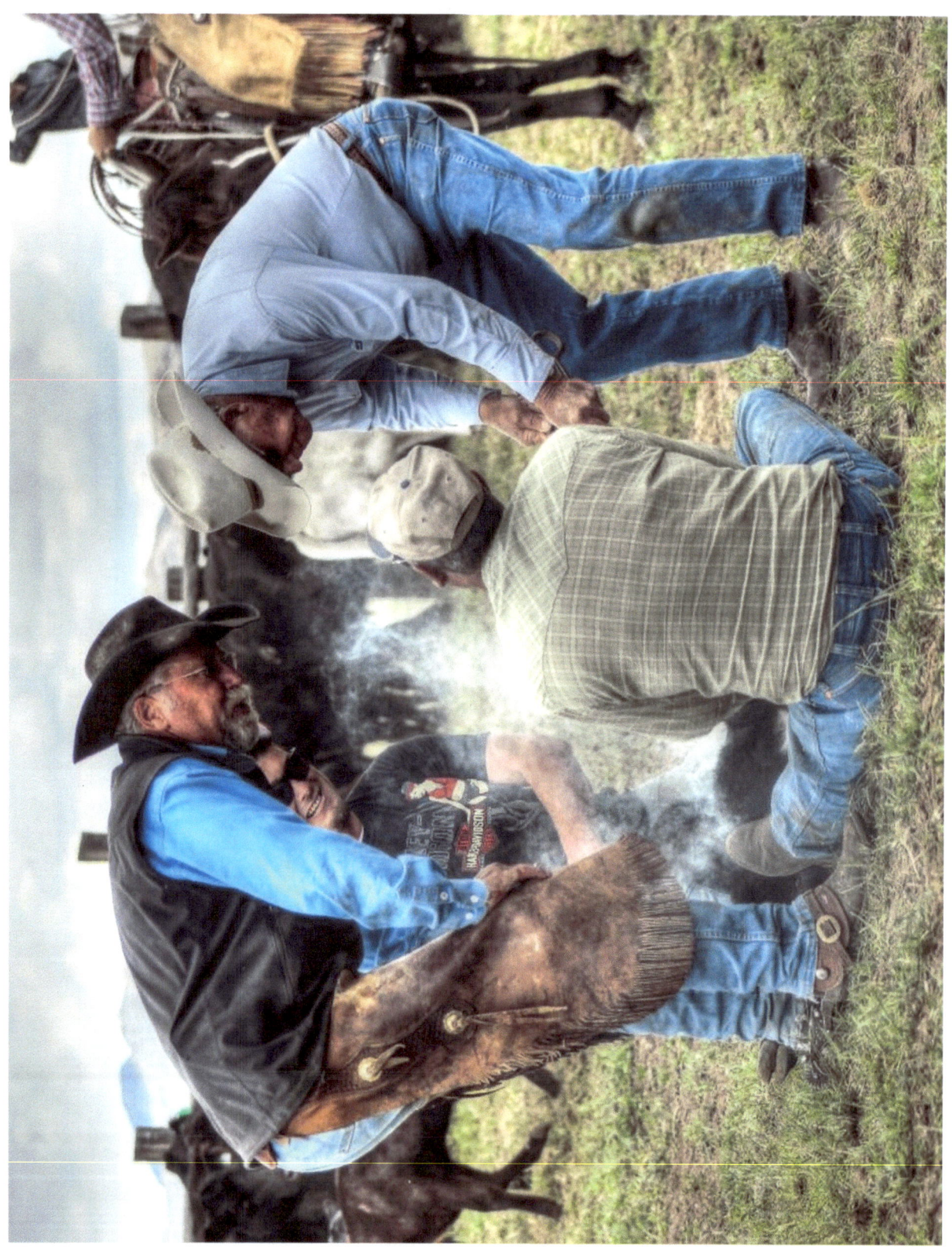

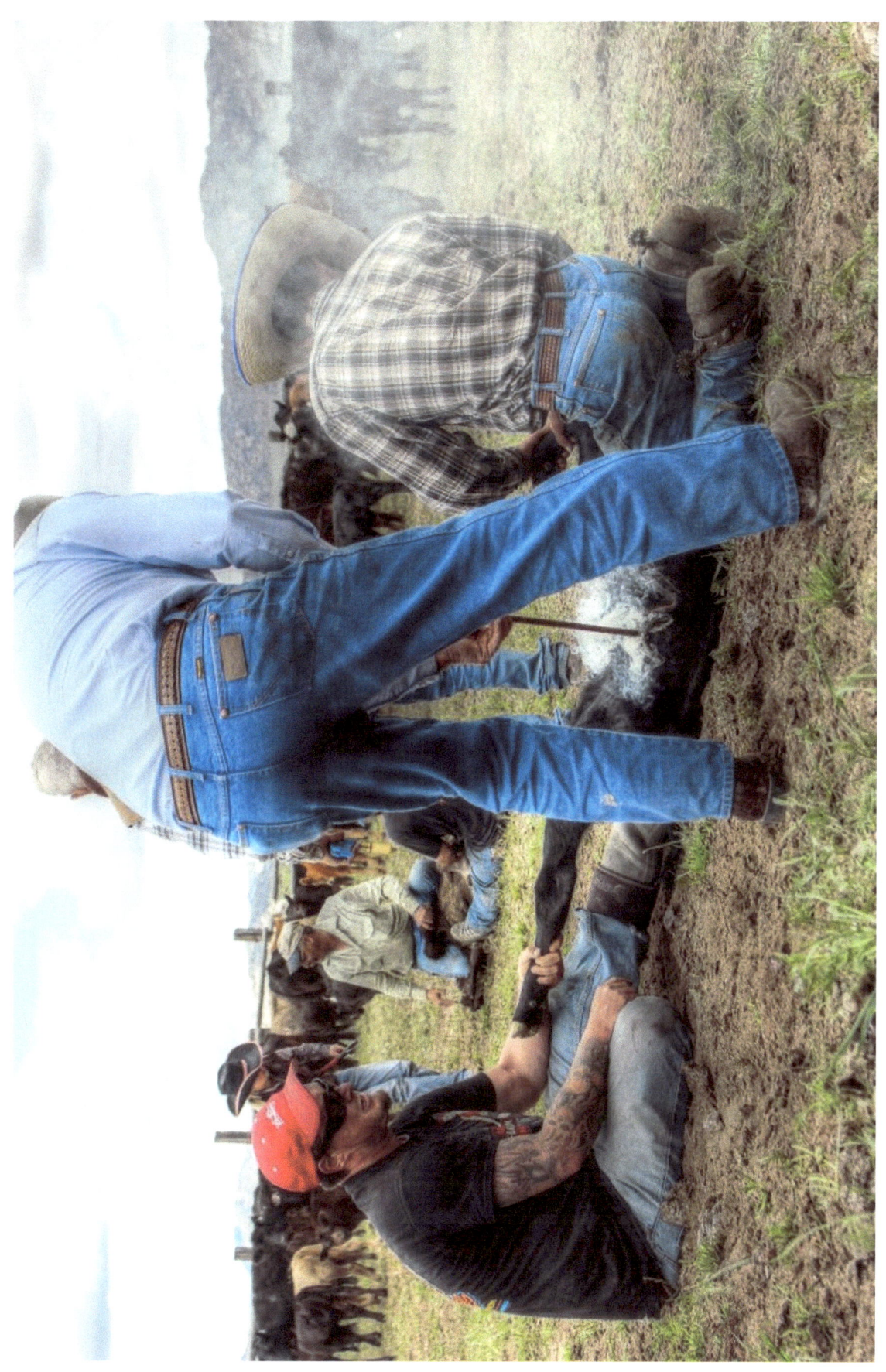

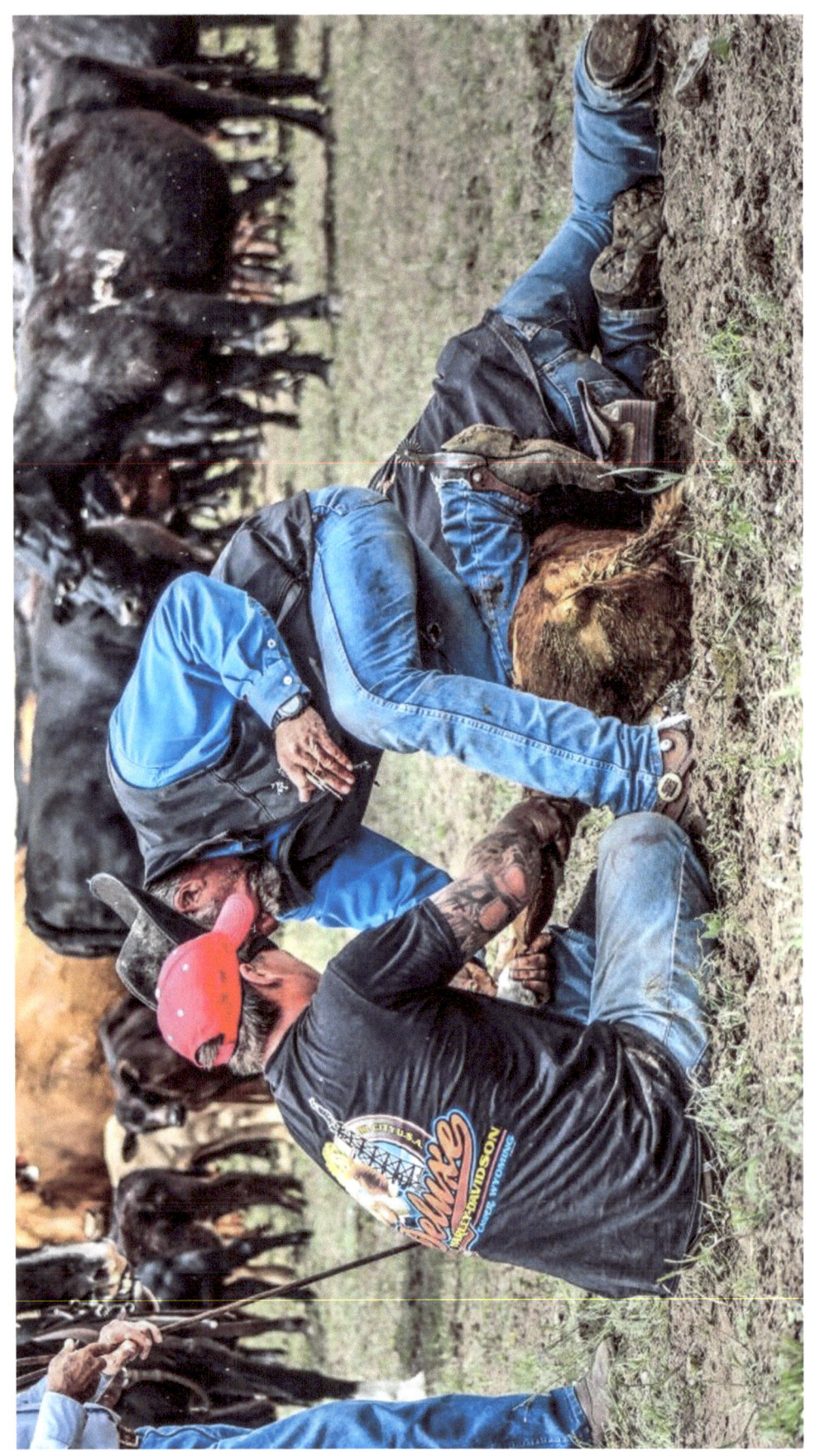

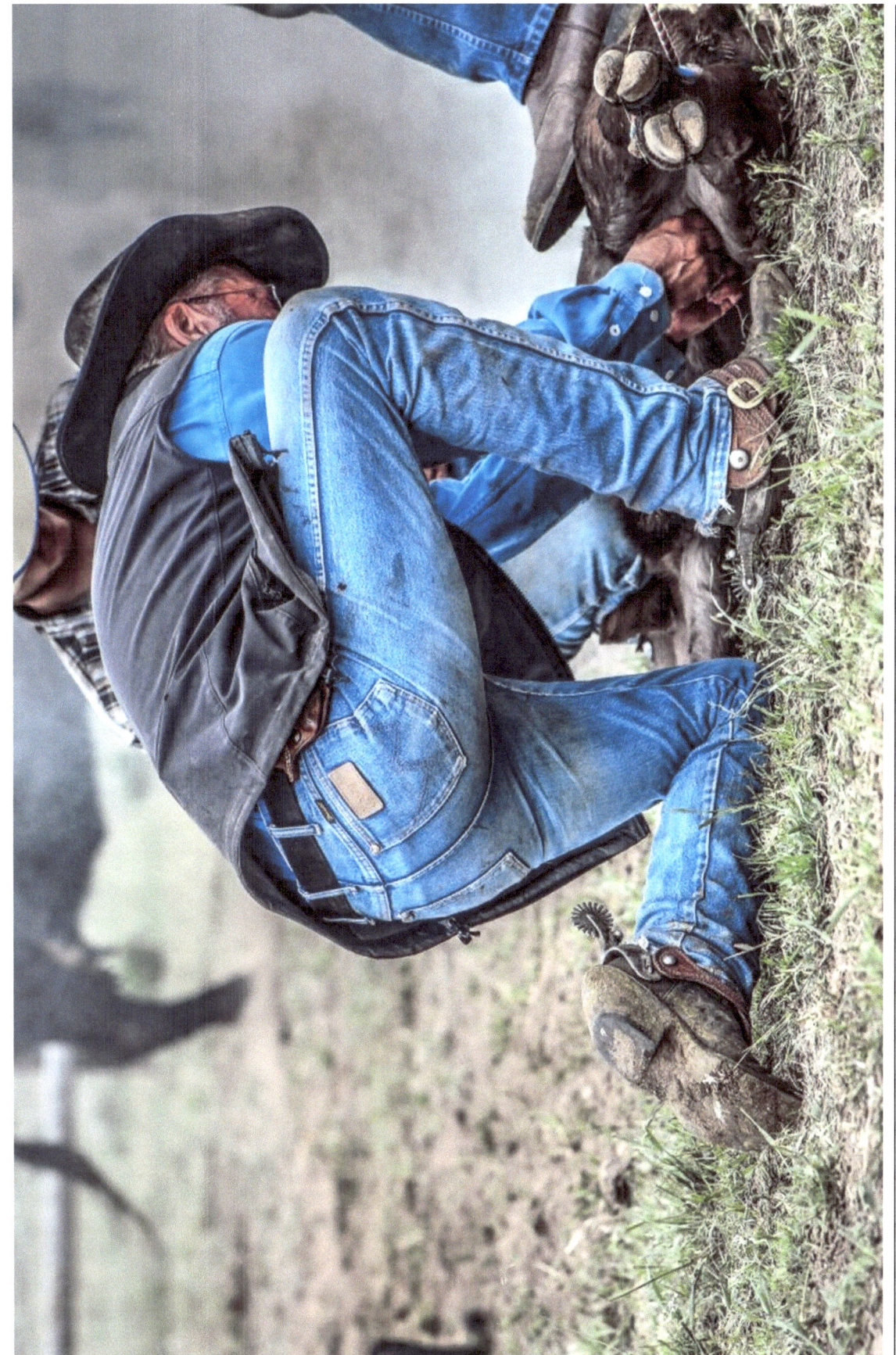

Castrating is one job that not just anyone is qualified to handle.

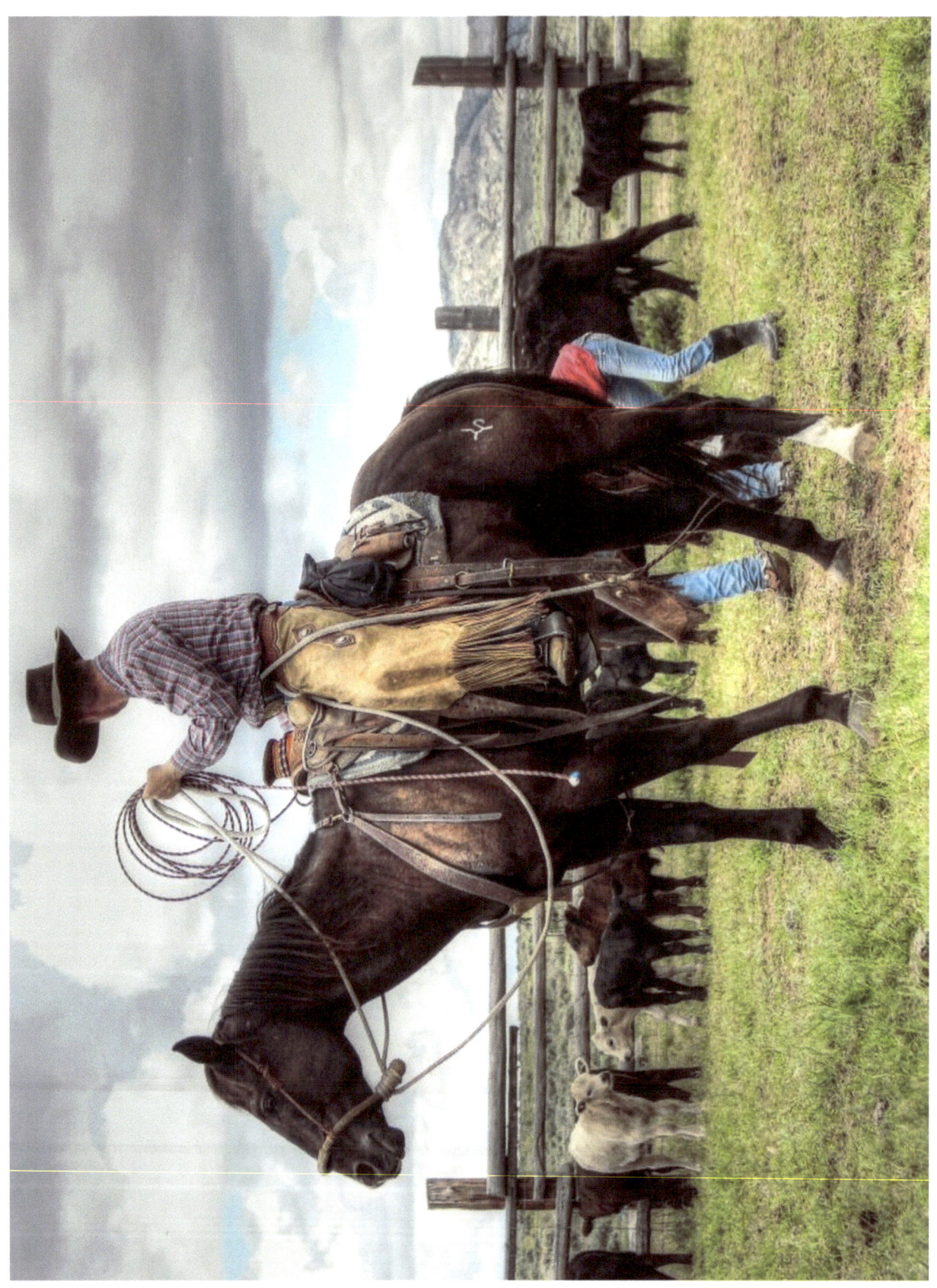

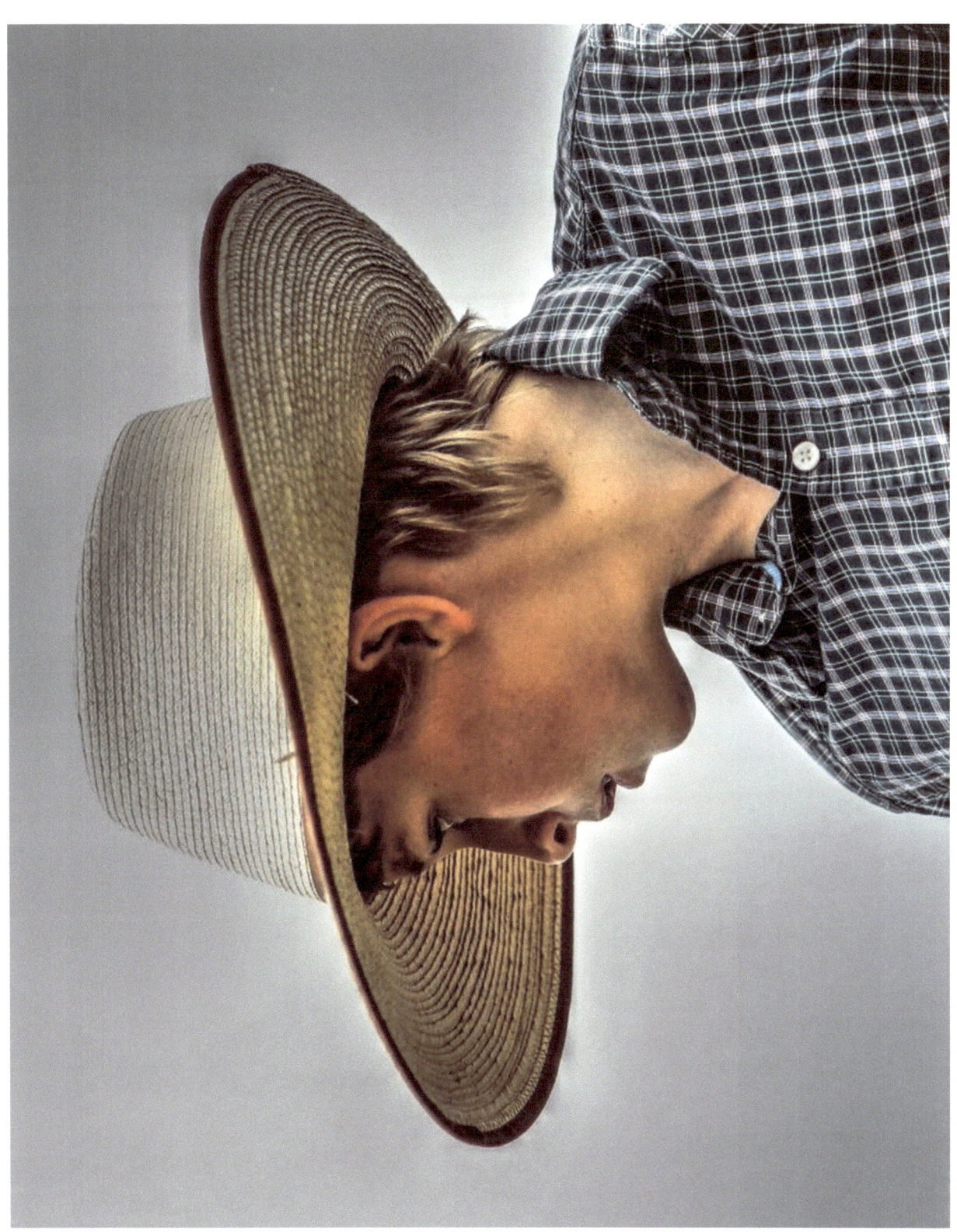

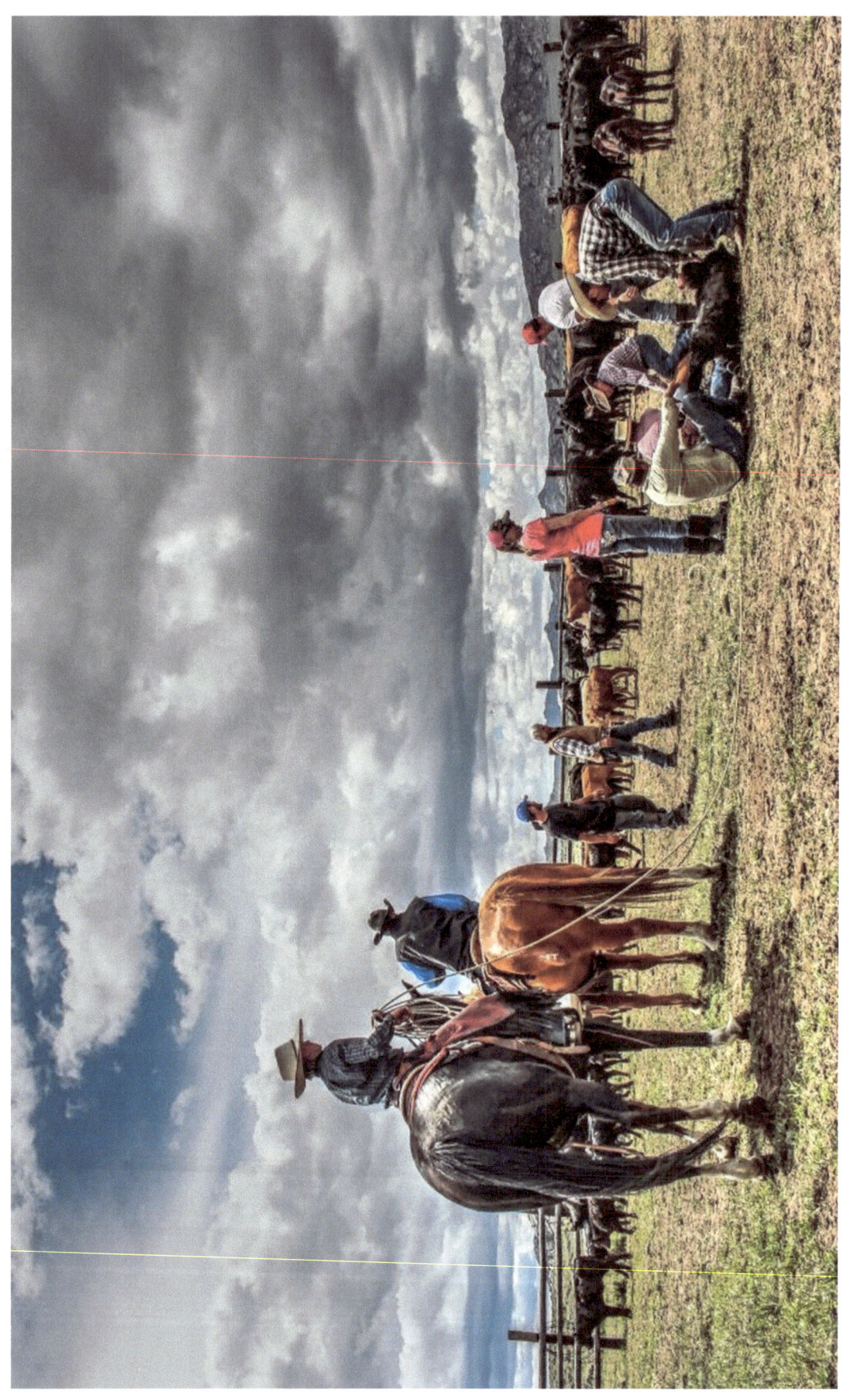

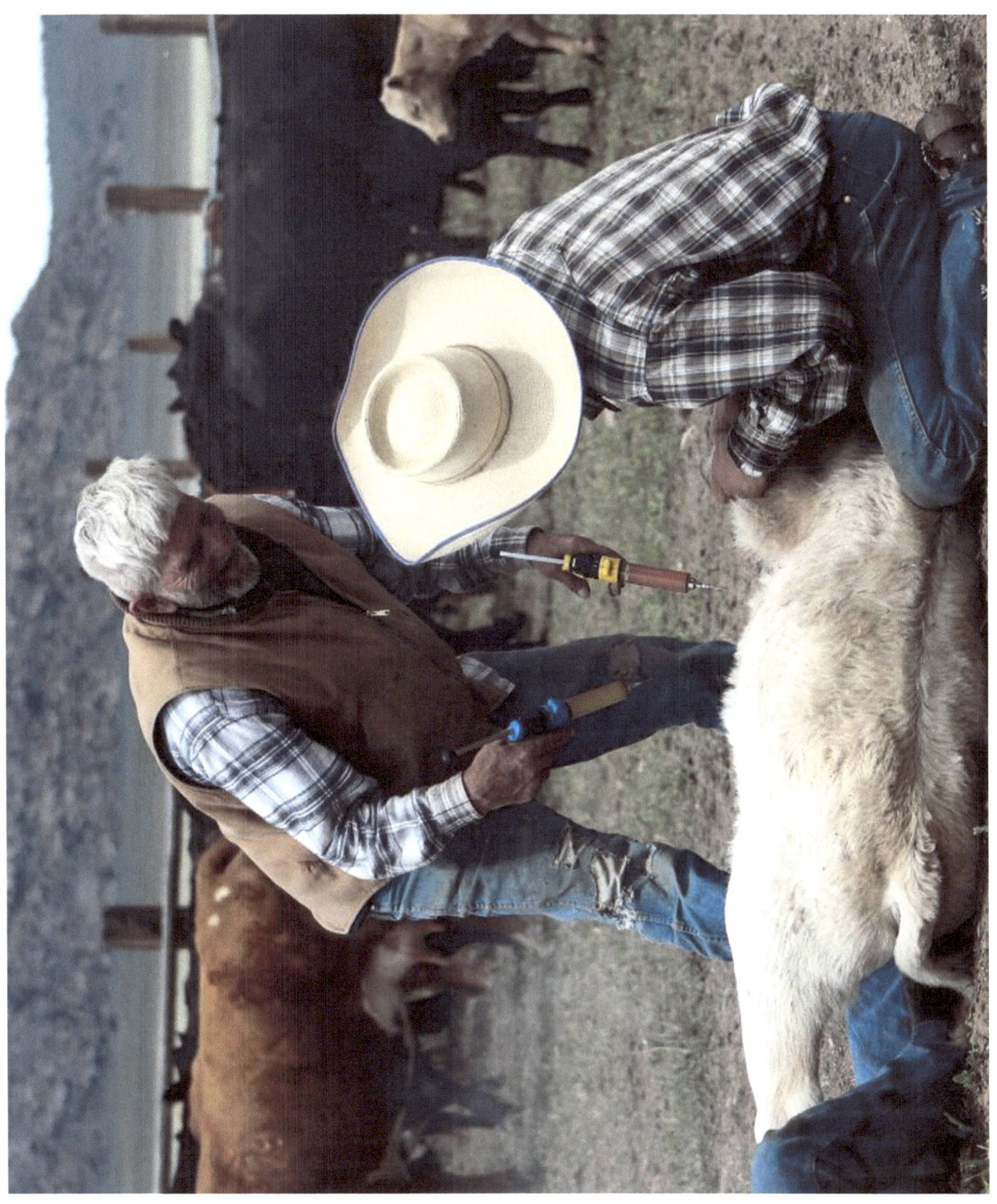

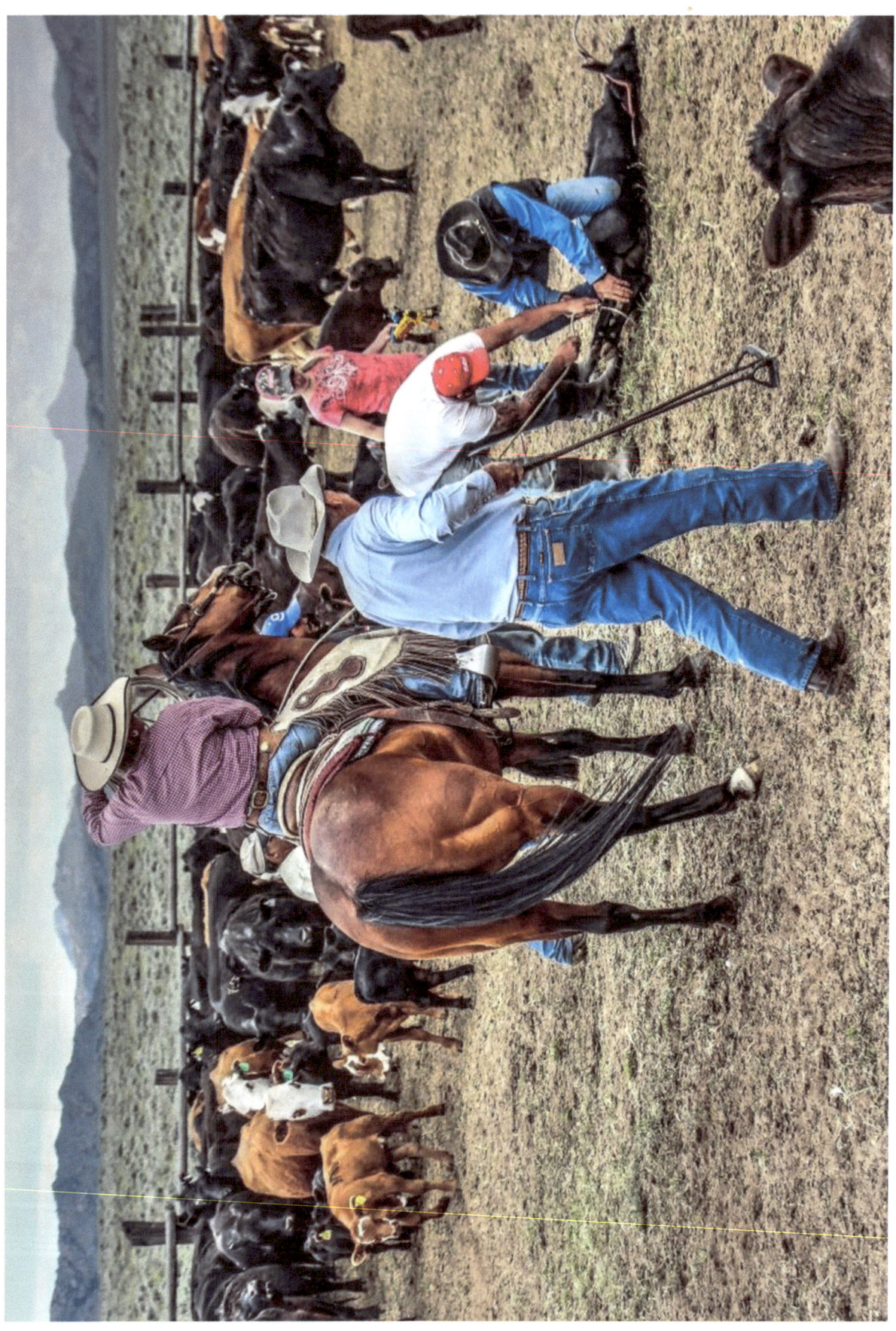

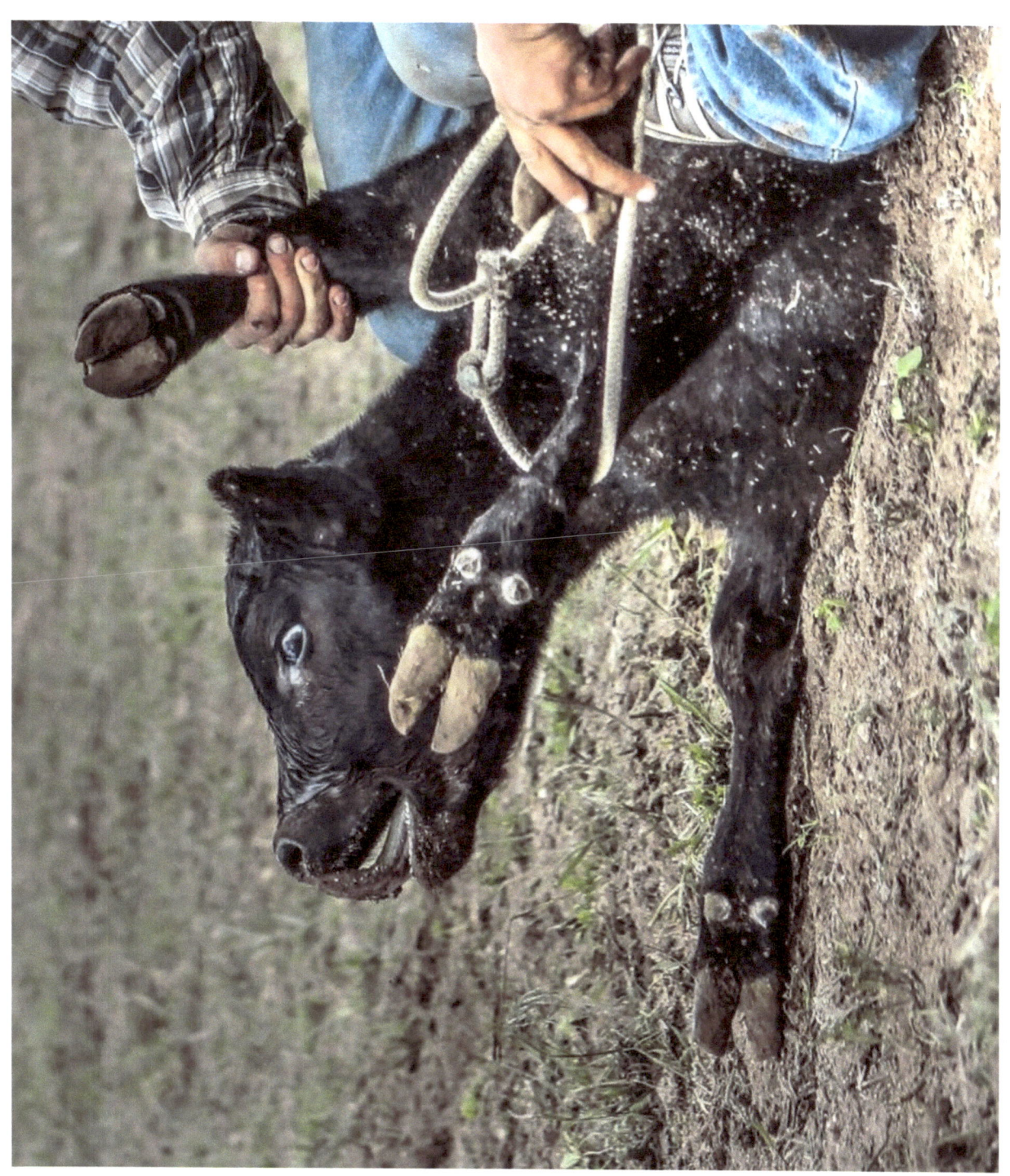

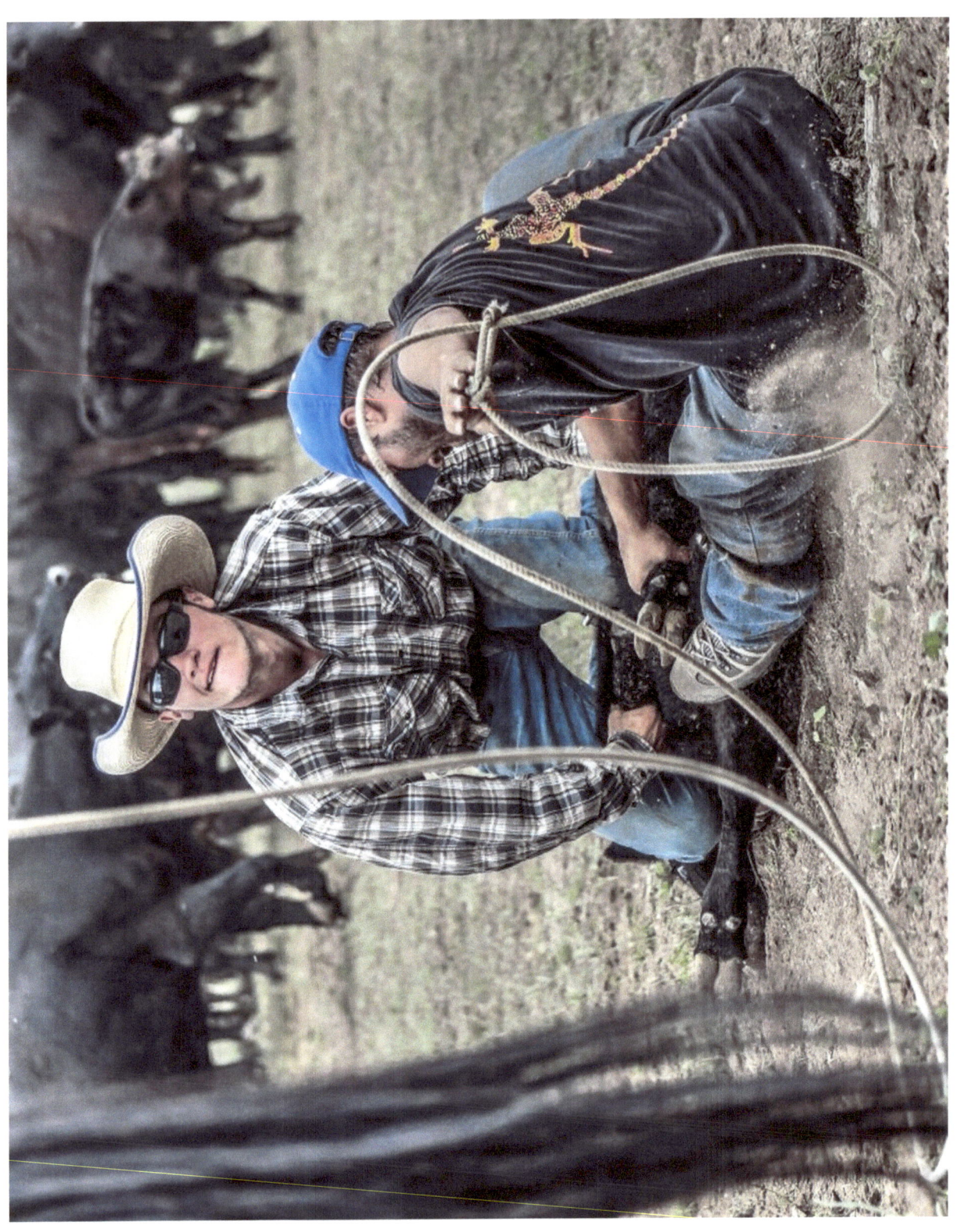

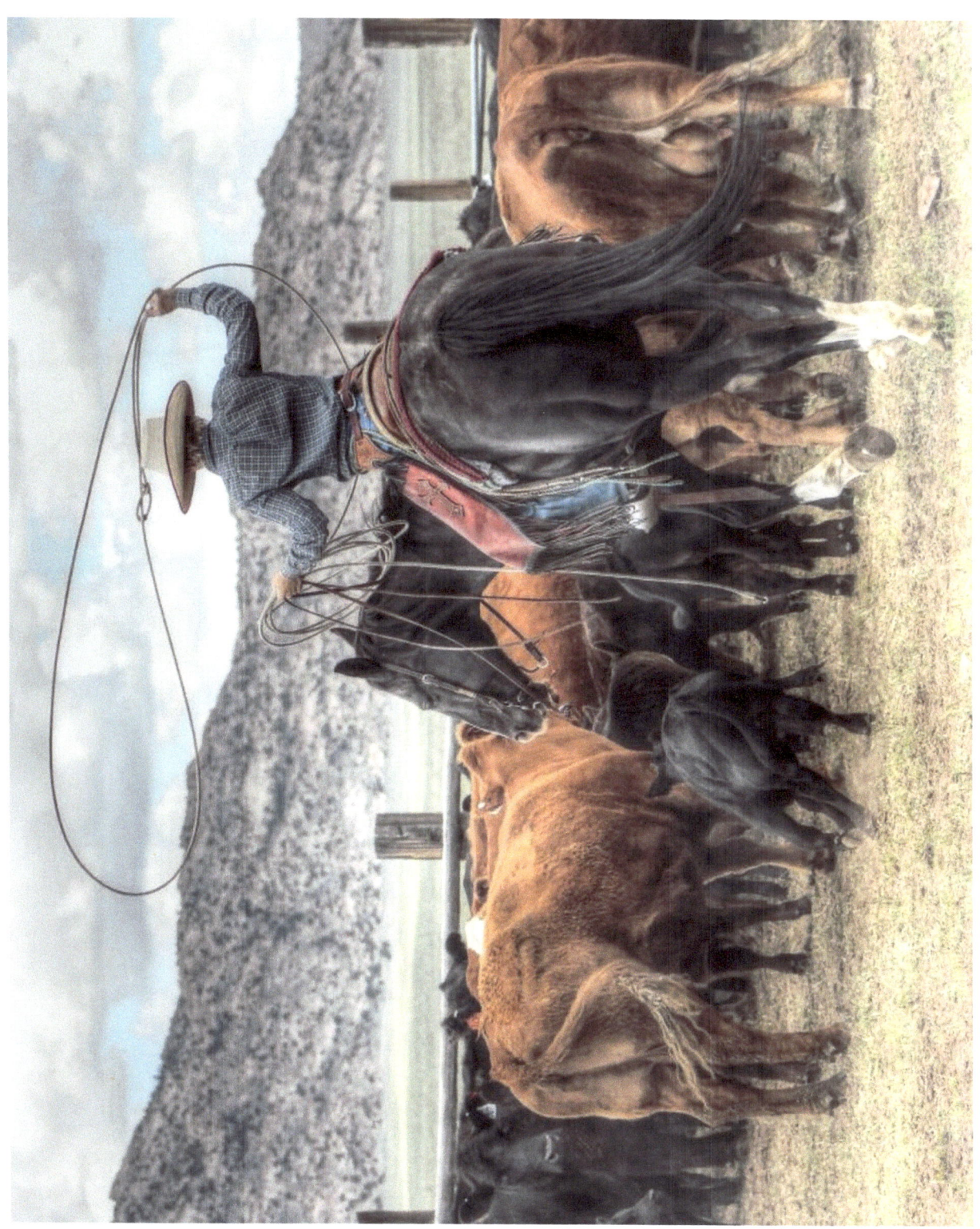

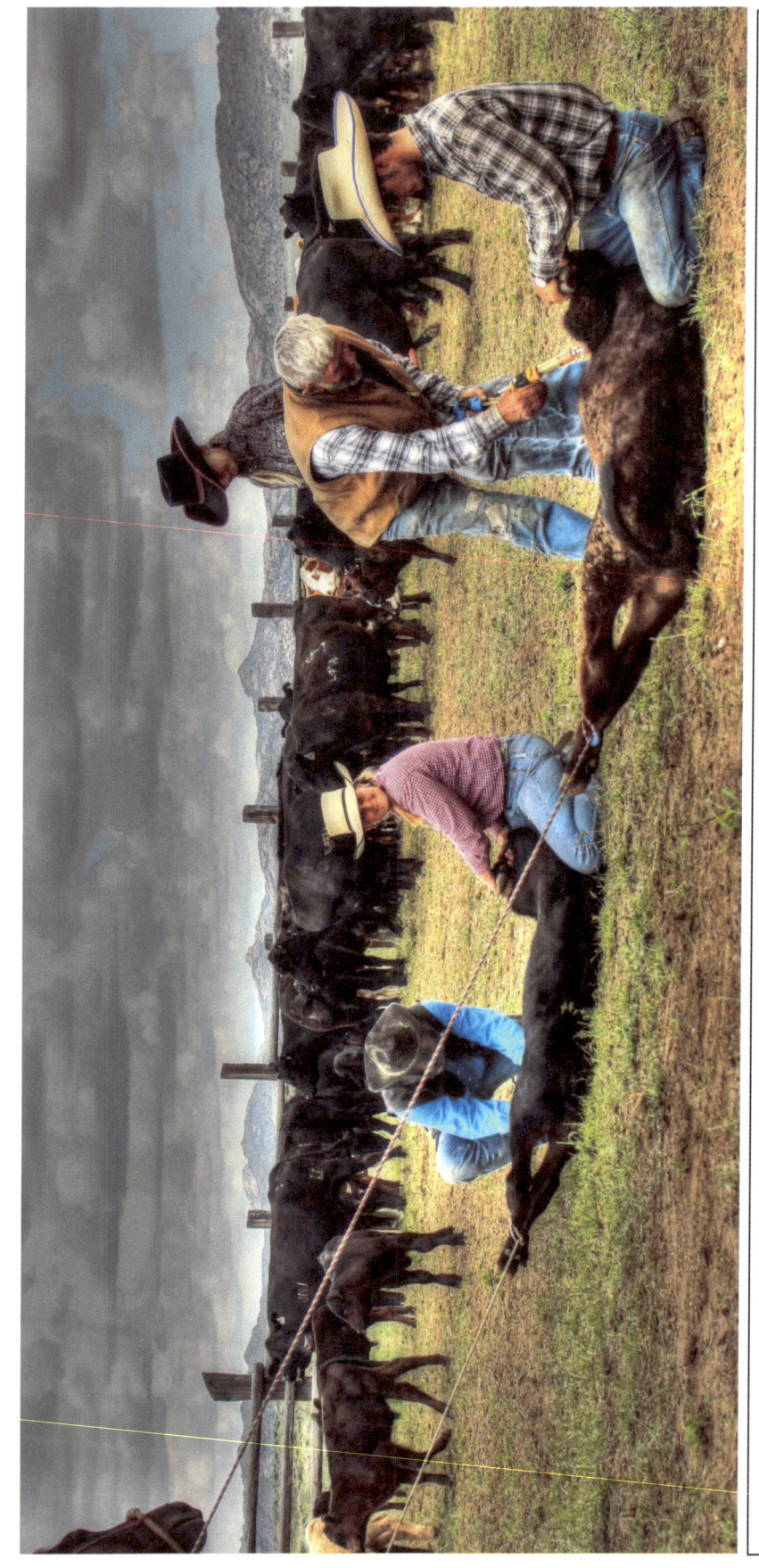

Jobs at a branding are NOT gender specific.

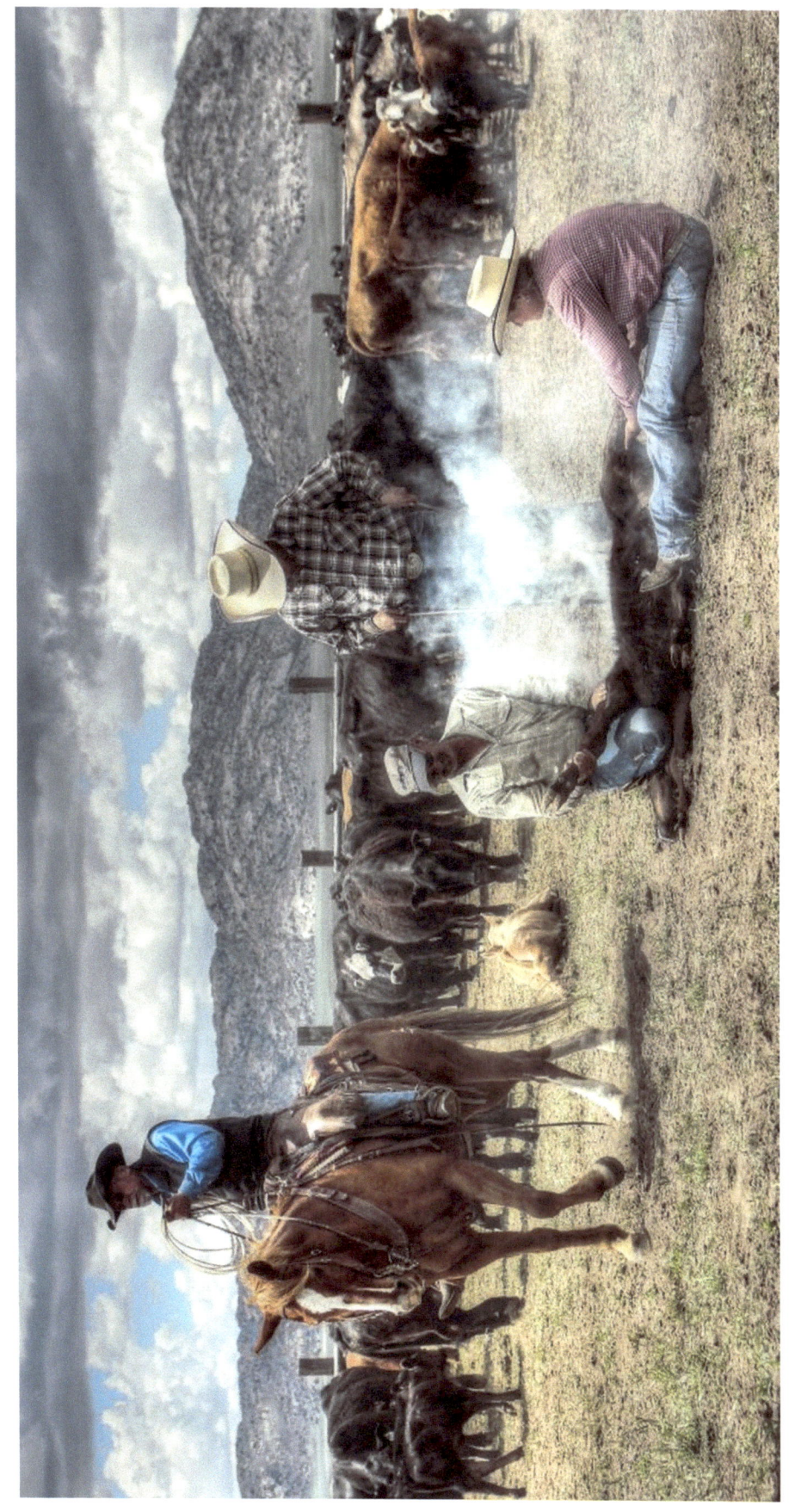

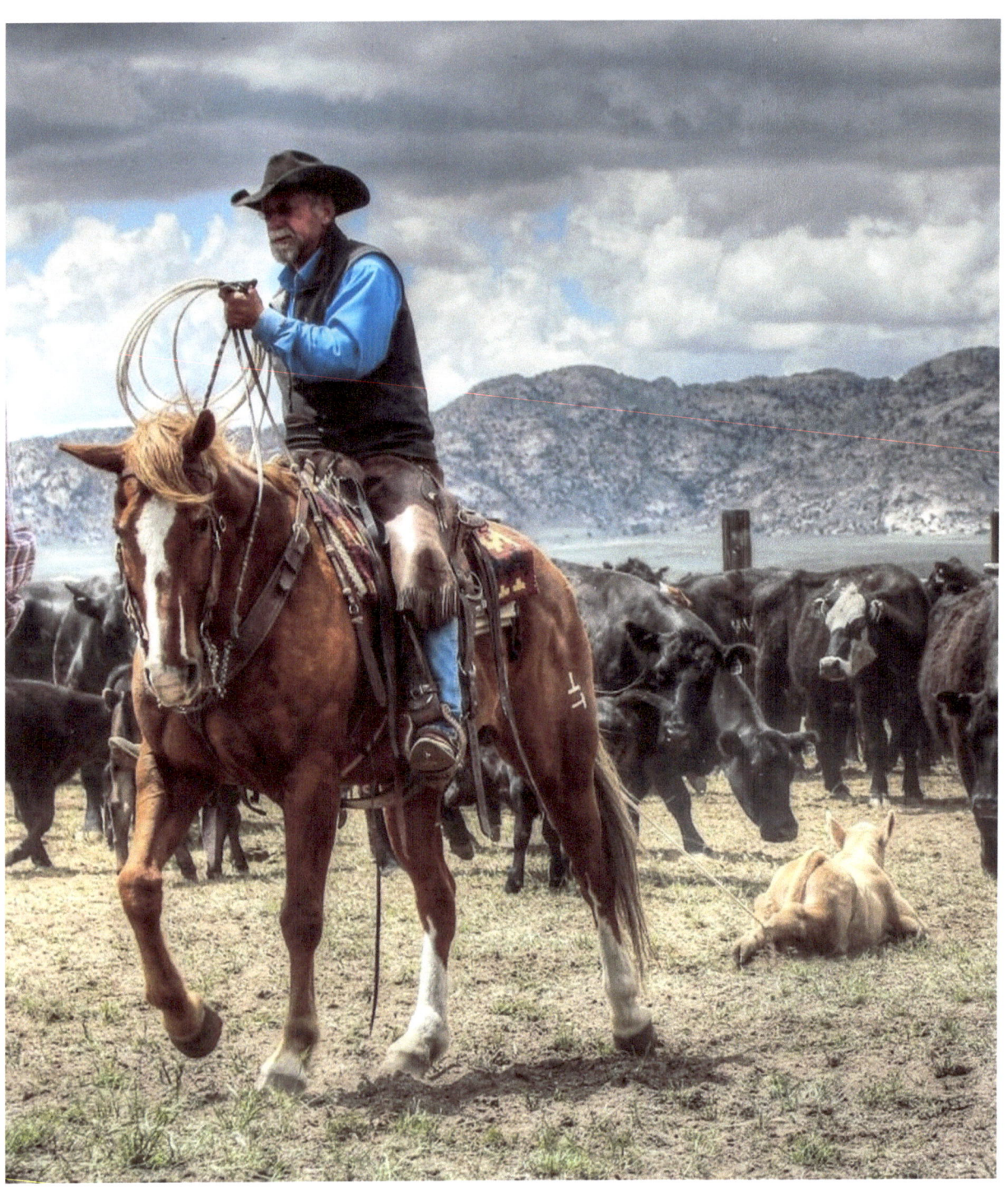

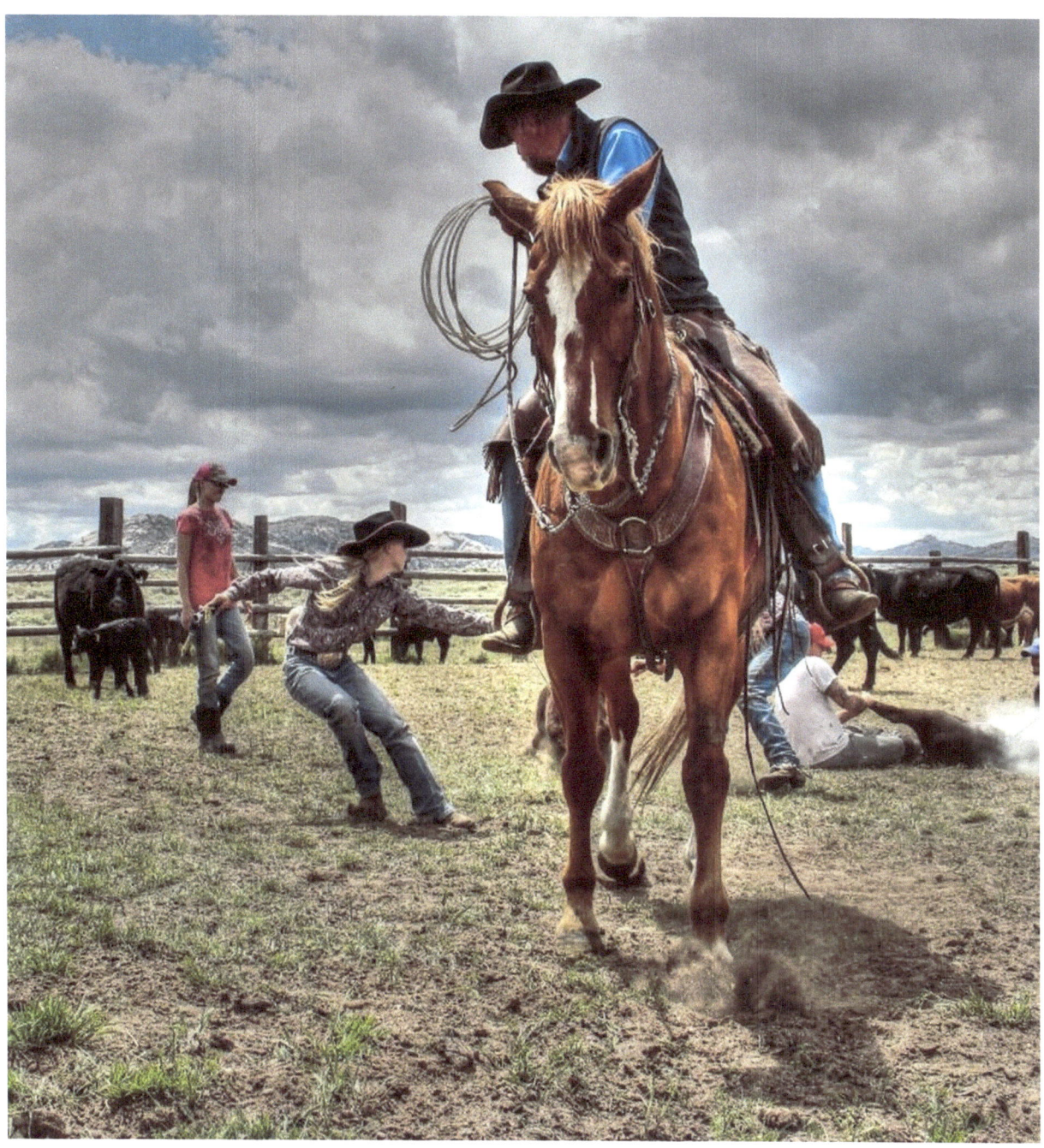

Most of the horses know their jobs as well as the cowhands know theirs.

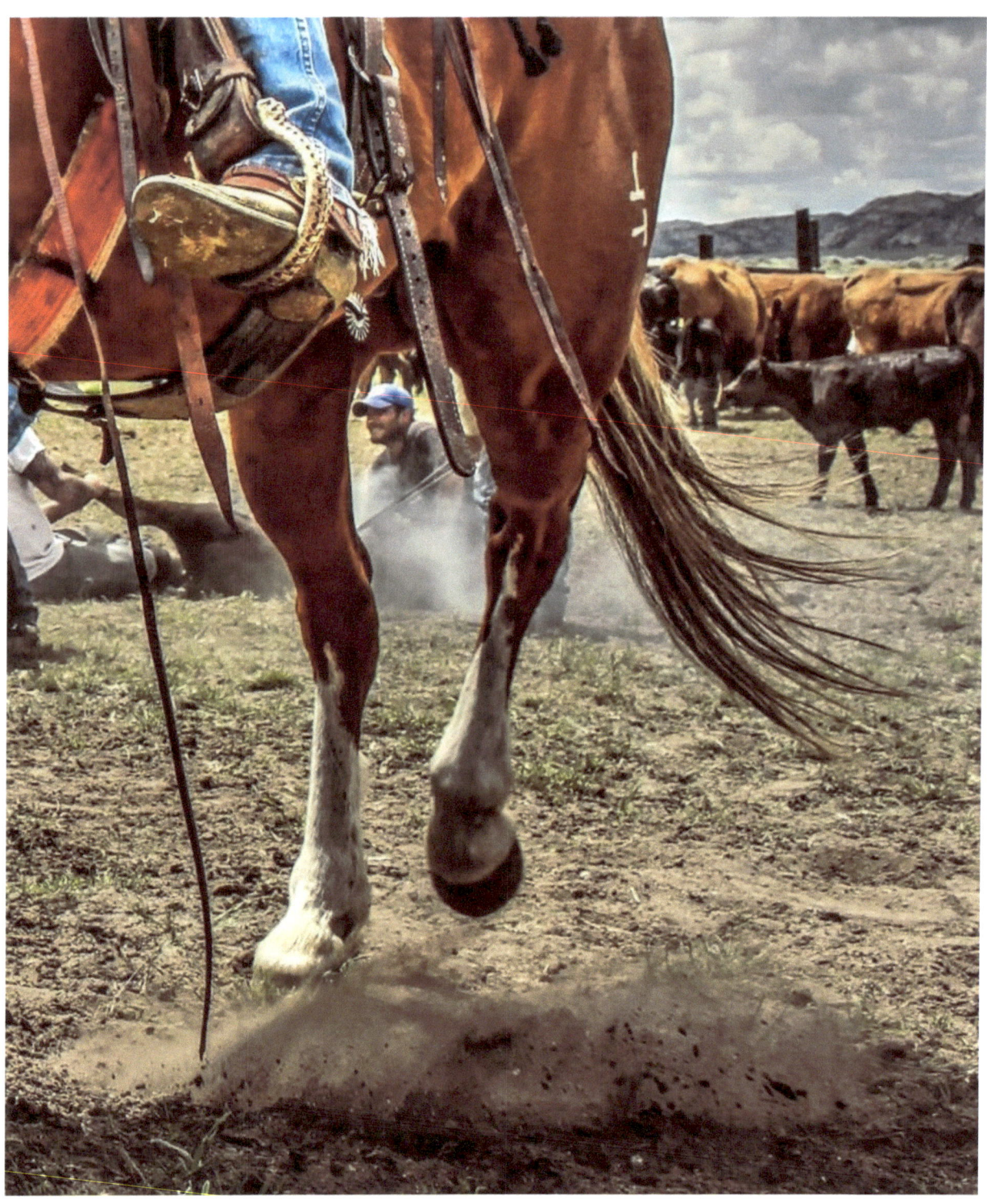

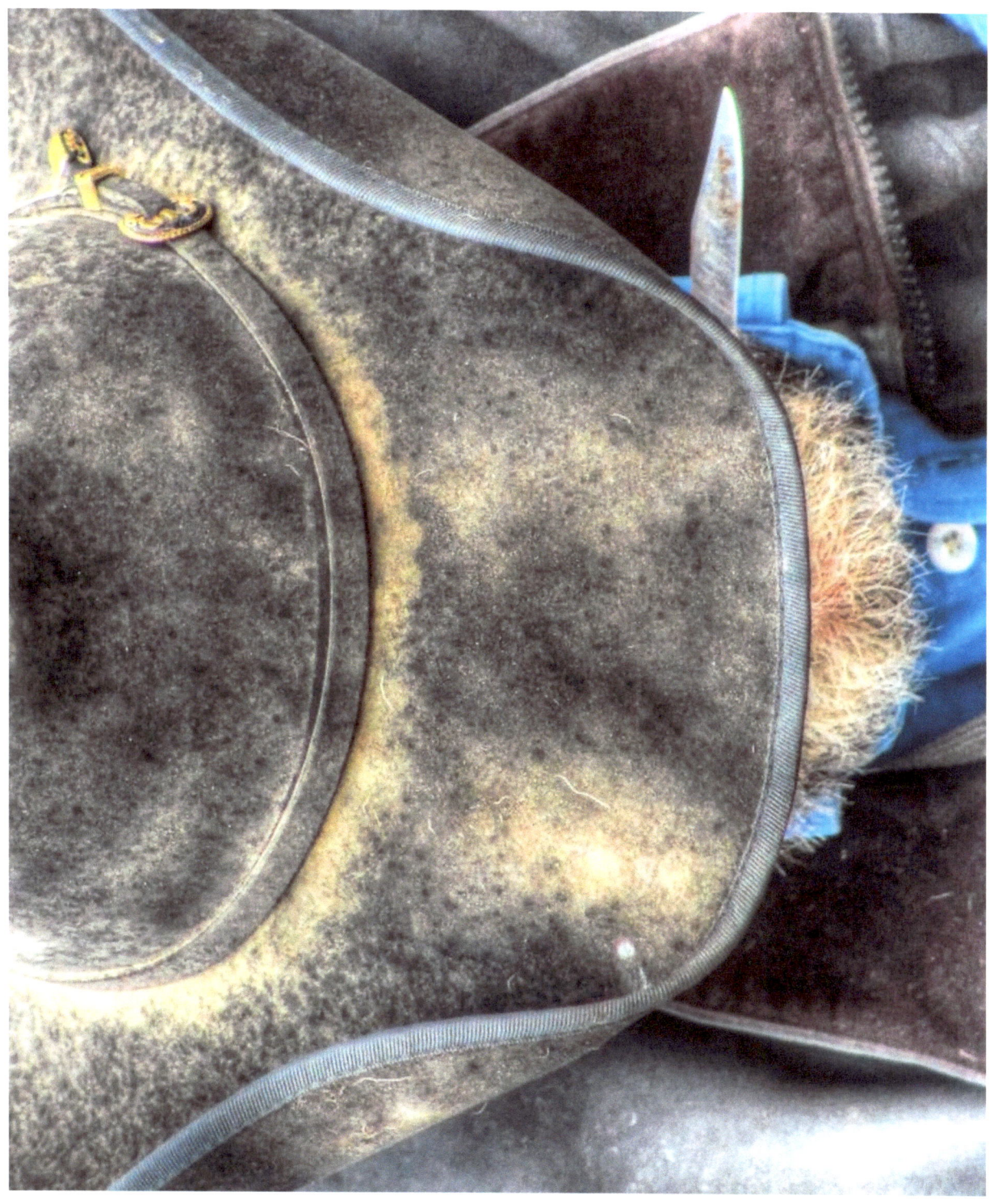

www.ingramcontent.com/pod-product-compliance
Lightning Source LLC
Chambersburg PA
CBHW050909180526
45159CB00007B/2846